COOL GUIDE
London

teNeues

Imprint

Editor: Martin Nicholas Kunz, Editorial coordination: Lea Bauer, Sabine Scholz

Photos (location): © 1707 Wine Bar at Fortnum & Mason (1707 Wine Bar at Fortnum & Mason), © Artesian Bar (Artesian Bar), Roland Bauer (Cocoon Restaurant, The Zetter Restaurant, Adventure Bar & Lounge, Artesian Bar, Mamounia Lounge, The Loft, Westbourne House, Bamford & Sons. pp. 4, 6, 11, 12 b. l., 14), © Boxwood Café (Boxwood Café), © Buddha Bar (Buddha Bar), Joseph Burns (Wahaca), Lidia Casas (Richmond Park, p. 162), Peter Clayman (Borough Market, Camden Market, Covent Garden, Daunt Books, Harrods, Rococo Chocolates, The Tea House, City Hall, Design Museum, Hayward Gallery, London Aquarium, Richmond Park, Tate Modern, The London Eye, The Regent's Park, Westminster Cathedral, pp. 5, 7 b. l., 8, 12 b. r.), © Coco de Mer (Coco de Mer), Simon Dean Photography (Fifteen, p. 3), Matthew Donaldson (Canteen Spitalfields), Katharina Feuer (Moro, Nicole's, Salt Yard, Tom's Delicatessen, p. 13), © Fortnum & Mason (Fortnum & Mason), Jean-Pierre Gabriel (Le Pain Quotidien), © Ghost Inc (Ghost Inc, pp. 7 b. r., 76), Vanessa Grobler (Canteen Spitalfields), © ReproReady.com Limited (Harrods), © Kengo Kuma & Associates (Sake No Hana), Martin Nicholas Kunz (Hakkasan), David Loftus, Artwork: Damian Hirst (St Alban, p. 9), © London Aquarium (London Aquarium), © Royal Opera House photo: Peter Mackertich (Royal Opera House), © 2009 Philip Meech and Tim Kavanagh. All rights reserved (National Geographic Store), Nigel Young/Foster + Partners and Foster + Partners as Architects (City Hall), © Nobu Berkeley ST (Nobu Berkeley ST), Susanne Olbrich (Covent Garden), Simon Phipps (Canteen Spitalfields), © Puma (Puma Store, p. 110), © Tate Modern (Tate Modern), Sven Thierhoff (National Geographic Store. p. 10), Karsten Thormaehlen (Shakespeare's Globe Theatre, Harrods), Heike Wild (Borough Market, Covent Garden)

Cover photo: Peter Clayman

Back cover photos from top to bottom (location): Joseph Burns (Wahaca), Peter Clayman (Rococo Chocolates), © ReproReady.com Limited (Harrods), Peter Clayman (City Hall)

Price categories: £ = reasonable, ££ = moderate, £££ = upscale, ££££ = expensive

Introduction, Texts: Constanze Junker, Layout & Pre-press, Imaging: fusion publishing, Translations: Connexus GmbH, Sprachentransfer, Berlin

Produced by fusion publishing GmbH, Berlin   www.fusion-publishing.com

Published by teNeues Publishing Group

teNeues Verlag Gmbh + Co. KG
Am Selder 37
47906 Kempen, Germany
Tel.: 0049-(0)2152-916-0
Fax: 0049-(0)2152-916-111
E-mail: books@teneues.de

Press department:
arehn@teneues.de
Tel.: 0049-2152-916-202

www.teneues.com

teNeues Publishing Company
16 West 22nd Street
New York, NY 10010, USA
Tel.: 001-212-627-9090
Fax: 001-212-627-9511

teNeues Publishing UK Ltd.
York Villa, York Road
Byfleet
KT14 7HX, Great Britain
Tel.: 0044-1932-403509
Fax: 0044-1932-403514

teNeues France S.A.R.L.
93, rue Bannier
45000 Orléans, France
Tel.: 0033-2-38541071
Fax: 0033-2-38625340

ISBN: 978-3-8327-9294-7

Bibliographic information published by the Deutsche Nationalbibliothek.

The Deutsche Nationalbibliothek lists this publication in the Deutsche Nationalbibliografie; detailed bibliographic data are available in the Internet at http://dnb.d-nb.de.

Introduction 6

RESTAURANTS & CAFÉS

Boxwood Café 16
Canteen Spitalfields 20
Cocoon Restaurant 24
Fifteen 28
Hakkasan 32
Le Pain Quotidien 36
Moro 40
Nicole's 44
Nobu Berkeley ST 48
Sake No Hana 52
Salt Yard 56
St Alban 60
The Zetter Restaurant 64
Tom's Delicatessen 68
Wahaca 72

CLUBS, LOUNGES & BARS

1707 Wine Bar 78
Adventure Bar & Lounge 82
Artesian Bar 86
Buddha Bar 90
Ghost Inc 94
Mamounia Lounge 98
The Loft 102
Westbourne House 106

SHOPS

Bamford & Sons 112
Borough Market 116
Camden Market 120
Coco de Mer 122
Covent Garden 126
Daunt Books 132
Fortnum & Mason 136
Harrods 140
National Geographic Store 146
Puma Store 150
Rococo Chocolates 154
The Tea House 158

HIGHLIGHTS

City Hall 164
Design Museum 168
Hayward Gallery 172
London Aquarium 176
Richmond Park 180
Royal Opera House 184
Shakespeare's Globe Theatre 188
Tate Modern 192
The London Eye 198
The Regent's Park 202
Westminster Cathedral 208

SERVICE

Service/Map 212

Introduction

Everyone senses it instantly – something is in the air! All London is humming and vibrating with life, opposites clash: tradition and modernity, past and present. On Westminster Bridge, the measured strokes of Big Ben mingle with the jangling of mobile phones. Great Britain may be located at the edge of Europe geographically and politically, but economically and culturally London has become the continent's de facto capital. Or perhaps even world leader in matters of business, finance, culture and cuisine?

The history of this city goes in phases: turbulent development is replaced by near standstill. The last time London was at the centre of interest was in the Swinging Sixties. Music and fashion cast their spell over an entire generation. Now its time has come again: London's art and theatre scene is again setting the trend today. The start of the new millennium appears to have inspired London; it is gripped by a building boom partly financed by state lottery funding.

However, the most striking feature is the change in London's population. They daily trans-form their vast metropolis into the most cosmopolitan on earth. Fifty nationalities and three hundred languages coexist, more than anywhere else in Europe – the whole world lives in London. Yet at the same time, the city seems more European than ever. Everything you might wish to be, every way of life you might wish to lead can be found here. London is the city of infinite possibilities.

Constanze Junker

Einleitung

Jeder spürt es sofort – hier liegt was in der Luft! Überall in London brodelt und vibriert das Leben, prallen die Gegensätze aufeinander: Tradition und Moderne, Geschichte und Gegenwart – das gemessene Schlagen von Big Ben mischt sich auf der Westminster Bridge mit dem Geklingel der Mobiltelefone. Großbritannien mag sich geografisch und politisch am Rande Europas befinden – wirtschaftlich und kulturell ist London de facto die Hauptstadt des Kontinents geworden. Oder doch gleich Weltspitze in Sachen Wirtschaft, Finanzen, Kultur und Kochkunst?

Die Geschichte dieser Stadt verläuft in Phasen – stürmische Entwicklung wird abgelöst durch Beinahe-Stillstand. Zuletzt stand London in den Swinging Sixties im Mittelpunkt des Interesses. Musik und Mode schlugen eine ganze Generation in ihren Bann. Jetzt ist es wieder soweit – von Londons Kunst- und Theaterszene gehen heute wieder richtungsweisende Impulse aus. Der Beginn des neuen Jahrtausends schien London zu beflügeln, es wurde von einem Bauboom gepackt, der zum Teil mit Mitteln aus der staatlichen Lotterie finanziert wurde.

Am auffallendsten aber haben sich Londons Menschen verändert. Sie verwandeln ihre Millionenstadt täglich in die kosmopolitischste der Erde. 50 Nationalitäten und 300 Sprachen nebeneinander, soviel wie sonst nirgendwo in Europa – in London lebt die ganze Welt. Und zugleich wirkt die Stadt europäischer denn je. Alles, was man sein möchte, jedes Leben, das man führen möchte: Hier kann man es finden. London ist die Stadt der unbegrenzten Möglichkeiten.

Constanze Junker

Introduction

Chacun le sent immédiatement – ici il y a quelque chose dans l'air ! A Londres, la vie bouillonne et vibre de toutes parts, les contraires coexistent et se heurtent tout à fois : tradition et modernité, histoire et présent – la sonnerie mesurée de Big Ben se mêle, sur le Westminster Bridge, aux appels incessants des portables. S'il est vrai que la Grande-Bretagne se trouve géographiquement et politiquement au bord de l'Europe, la ville de Londres est devenue, de fait, la capitale du continent aussi bien sur le plan culturel qu'économique. Mieux encore : n'occupe-t-elle pas une place internationale de premier plan dans les domaines de l'économie, des finances, de la culture et des arts culinaires?

L'histoire de cette ville se déroule par phases successives – un développement foudroyant laisse souvent place à une période d'évolution lente, presque d'arrêt. Dernièrement, durant les Swinging Sixties, Londres occupait le devant de la scène. La musique et la mode de cette époque fascinèrent toute une génération. Maintenant ce phénomène se renouvelle – les impulsions d'avenir partent aujourd'hui de nouveau des milieux londoniens de l'art et du théâtre. Le début du nouveau millénaire semble avoir stimulé Londres : la capitale de l'Angleterre a été entraînée dans un boom du bâtiment financé, en partie, grâce aux moyens fournis par la loterie nationale.

Mais se sont surtout les habitants de Londres qui paraissent avoir changé de la façon la plus frappante. Chaque jour, ils transforment leur ville comptant plusieurs millions d'habitants en une capitale mondiale du cosmopolitisme. 50 nationalités et près de 300 langues différentes se côtoient. Plus que partout ailleurs en Europe – des personnes venues du monde entier vivent à Londres. Et, en, même temps, la ville porte plus que jamais l'empreinte de l'Europe. On peut rencontrer ici toutes les façons d'être et tous les types de vies possibles et imaginables. Londres est la ville des possibilités illimitées.

Constanze Junker

...o el mundo lo percibe enseguida: ¡hay algo que flota en el ambiente! En cualquier pun-
...de la ciudad de Londres bulle y vibra la vida, chocando entre sí los extremos: tradición y
...odernidad, pasado y presente; las comedidas campanadas del Big Ben se mezclan sobre
...el Westminster Bridge con los sonidos de los teléfonos móviles. Aunque Gran Bretaña
pueda encontrarse, tanto geográfica como políticamente, en los confines de Europa, ello
no obsta para que Londres se haya convertido de facto, desde un punto de vista económi-
co y cultural, en la capital del continente. ¿O incluso en el centro mundial en cuestiones
económicas, financieras, culturales y gastronómicas?

La historia de esta ciudad se desarrolla por fases: a fases de impetuoso desarrollo le
siguen otras de paralización o inacción casi completa. Londres se situó durante la Swinging Sixties en el centro de interés. La música y la moda cautivaron a toda una generación.
Ahora se vuelve a repetir esta situación; de la escena teatral y artística parten actualmente
impulsos que marcan la pauta. El inicio del nuevo siglo parece haber dado alas a Londres
que ha experimentado un boom de la construcción que se ha financiado en parte con
medios procedentes de la lotería estatal.

Lo más llamativo es, no obstante, la transformación que han experimentado los habitantes
de Londres. Diariamente convierten su ciudad de millones de habitantes en la más cosmopolita de la tierra. En ella conviven 50 nacionalidades y 300 idiomas, más que en ningún
otro lugar de Europa; en Londres vive el mundo entero. Y al mismo tiempo ofrece la ciudad
un aspecto más europeo que nunca. Aquí se puede encontrar todo lo que uno quiera ser o
la vida que uno desee vivir. Londres es la ciudad de las oportunidades ilimitadas.

Constanze Junker

RESTAURANTS & CAFÉS

Boxwood Café

The Berkeley
Wilton Place
London, SW1X 7RL
Knightsbridge
Phone: +44 / 20 / 72 35 10 10
www.gordonramsay.com

Opening hours: Mon–Fri noon to 3 pm, 6 pm to 1 am, Sat+Sun noon to 4 pm, 6 pm to 11 pm
Prices: £££
Cuisine: British
Tube: Victoria Station, Knightsbridge, Hyde Park Corner, Sloane Square
Map: No. 1

This restful oasis in the hectic pace of Knightsbridge with its elegant, stylish interior stands for informal indulgence. The bar's lime green and dark chocolate brown finish exudes the flair of British nobility. Offering relaxed but informal dining emphasising British produce of the highest order with seasonal ingredients freshly sourced and presented from the daily market menu.

Diese erholsame Oase in der Hektik Knightsbridges steht mit ihrem eleganten, stylishen Interieur für ungezwungenen Genuss. Die lindgrüne und zartbitterbraune Ausstattung der Bar atmet das Flair britischer Noblesse. Hier werden in entspannter und zwangloser Atmosphäre Speisen geboten, die den Fokus auf britische Produkte höchster Güte legen, zubereitet mit frischen saisonalen Zutaten, die das tägliche Marktangebot bietet.

Ce havre de paix au milieu de la fébrilité du Knightsbridge permet de goûter aux délices de la cuisine dans une ambiance décontractée. La décoration du bar, vert tilleul et d'un marron à la fois tendre et acide fait revivre le charme de la noblesse britannique. Dans une atmosphère relaxante et sans cérémonie, l'accent est mis sur des produits anglais de première qualité, préparés avec des aliments frais de saison offerts chaque jour sur les marchés.

Este oasis reparador en medio del ajetreo de Knightsbridge ofrece, con su interior de estilo elegante, la posibilidad de disfrutar de manera informal. La decoración del Bar de color verde pálido y marrón suave respira el ambiente de la Noblesse británica. En este local, y en un ambiente relajado e informal, se ofrecen platos que se centran fundamentalmente en productos británicos de máxima calidad, preparándose con ingredientes frescos de temporada que se hallan diariamente disponibles en el mercado.

Canteen Spitalfields

2 Crispin Place
London, E1 6DW
Spitalfields
Phone: +44 / 845 / 6 86 11 22
www.canteen.co.uk

Opening hours: Mon–Fri 8 am to 11 pm, Sat+Sun 9 am 11 pm
Prices: ££
Cuisine: Modern British
Tube: Aldgate East, Liverpool Street, Aldgate
Map: No. 2

Canteen offers traditional favourites and modernised classics of British cuisine in a contemporary and friendly ambience. An unusual concept forms its basis: The voluntary commitment to the creation of good, honest food made from fresh, seasonal ingredients, nationally sourced and reasonably priced. Apparently, the breakfast here is one of the best in Britain.

Das Canteen bietet traditionelle Favoriten und modernisierte Klassiker der britischen Küche in einem zeitgemäßen und freundlichen Ambiente. Ein ungewöhnliches Konzept bildet seine Basis: Die Selbst-verpflichtung zur sorgfältigen Herstellung von gutem, ehrlichem Essen aus frischen, saisonalen Zutaten nationaler Herkunft zu einem angemessenen Preis. Eines der besten Frühstücke in Großbritannien soll es hier geben.

Le Canteen offre les mets favoris traditionnels mais aussi des classiques modernisés de la cuisine britannique dans une ambiance moderne et conviviale. Les bases d'une telle réussite ? Une concep-tion qui sort de l'ordinaire : le restaurant s'engage à préparer soigneusement de bons repas, à partir d'aliments frais de la saison, d'origine anglaise et à un prix raisonnable. C'est ici que l'on peut déguster un des meilleurs petits-déjeuners de la Grande-Bretagne.

El Canteen ofrece platos favoritos tradicionales y platos clásicos modernizados de la cocina inglesa dentro de un ambiente actual y agradable. Se basa en un concepto inusual: el compromiso contraído consigo mismo de preparar cuidadosamente unas excelentes comidas a partir de productos frescos, de temporada, de procedencia nacional, por un precio razonable. En él puede tomarse uno de los mejores almuerzos de toda Gran Bretaña.

Cocoon Restaurant

65 Regent Street
London, W1B 4EA
Westminster
Phone: +44 / 20 / 74 94 76 00
www.cocoon-restaurants.com

Opening hours: Mon–Fri noon to 3 pm, 5.30 pm to 1 am,
Sat 5.30 pm to 3 am, Late Lounge: Thu–Sat 11 pm to 3 am
Prices: ££
Cuisine: Pan Asian
Tube: Piccadilly
Map: No. 3

The Cocoon in Regent Street has received many awards for its design and atmosphere, and is considered to be one of London's most exclusive and fashionable venues. Carefully preserved traditions of Japanese, Chinese and Thai cuisines are blended here into refined, modern Pan-Asian creations. From 11 pm on Thursdays to Saturdays, the exquisitely styled restaurant is transformed into a Late Lounge.

Vielfach preisgekrönt für sein Design und die Atmosphäre gilt das Cocoon in der Regent Street als einer der exklusivsten und angesagtesten Treffpunkte Londons. Achtsam bewahrte Traditionen aus den Küchen Japans, Chinas und Thailands werden hier zu feinen, modernen Pan-Asian-Kreationen verbunden. Donnerstags bis samstags ab 23 Uhr wandelt sich das exquisit gestylte Restaurant zur Late Lounge.

Le Cocoon auquel plusieurs prix ont déjà été décernés en raison de son design et son atmosphère se trouve dans la Regent Street. Il a la réputation d'être l'un des rendez-vous les plus tendances et les plus sélects de Londres. Les traditions soigneusement préservées de la cuisine japonaise, chinoise et thaïlandaise sont synthétisées sous la forme de créations pan asiatiques modernes et raffinées. Du jeudi au samedi, à partir de 23 heures, ce restaurant, au style distingué, se transforme en « Late Lounge ».

El restaurante Cocoon situado en la Regent Street y premiado en repetidas ocasiones por su diseño y por su atmósfera es considerado como uno de los puntos de encuentro más exclusivos y apreciados de Londres. Unas tradiciones cuidadosamente mantenidas de las cocinas de Japón, China y Tailandia se combinan en este lugar con creaciones finas, modernas, del conjunto de Asia. A partir del jueves y hasta el sábado se transforma este local, a partir de las 23 horas, para convertirse el restaurante de estilo exquisito en Late Lounge.

Fifteen

15 Westland Place
London, N1 7LP
Hackney
Phone: +44 / 870 / 7 87 15 15
www.fifteen.net

Opening hours: Trattoria: breakfast Mon–Sat 7.30 am to 11 am, Sun 8 am to 11 am, lunch
Mon–Sat noon to 3 pm, Sun noon to 3.30 pm, dinner Mon–Sat 6 pm to 10 pm, Sun 6 pm to 9.30 pm
Prices: ££
Cuisine: Italian & Mediterranean
Tube: Old Street   **Map:** No. 4

Lydia Hearst's Special Tip
I strongly recommend the six-course tasting menu. You will not be disappointed.

A top restaurant and at the same time an opportunity for socially disadvantaged young people – Jamie
Oliver realised both aspects in one project in 2002. This restaurant presents itself at London's Westland
Place symbiotically with a trattoria and a dining room on two levels. In the open kitchen amazing dishes
are prepared with choice seasonal produce, care and enthusiasm – Mediterranean and extravagant
with an Italian flavour.

Ein Toprestaurant und zugleich eine Chance für sozial benachteiligte Jugendliche – Jamie Oliver verwirk-
lichte 2002 beide Aspekte in einem Projekt. Dieses präsentiert sich am Londoner Westland Place mit
einer Trattoria und einem Dining Room symbiotisch auf zwei Ebenen. In der offenen Küche werden mit
ausgesuchten saisonalen Produkten, Sorgfalt und Begeisterung erstaunliche Gerichte zubereitet –
mediterran und extravagant mit italienischem Touch.

Un restaurant de premier choix qui offre en même temps une chance à des jeunes gens socialement
désavantagés. En 2002, Jamie Oliver a su allier ces deux aspects dans un seul projet. Celui-ci se présente
sous la forme d'une symbiose au Westland Place qui comprend une Trattoria et un Dining Room. Dans la
cuisine des plats étonnants sont préparés avec soin et enthousiasme à partir de produits de saison minu-
tieusement choisis. Leur goût méditerranéen relevé d'originalité est marqué par un caractère italien.

Un restaurante de primera categoría que ofrece al mismo tiempo una oportunidad a jóvenes social-
mente discriminados; Jamie Oliver consiguió combinar en 2002 ambos aspectos en un proyecto. Dicho
proyecto se presentó en el Westland Place londinense a través de la simbiosis en dos niveles de una
Trattoria y un Dining Room. En la cocina abierta se preparan manjares extraordinarios con productos se-
leccionados de temporada, esmero e ilusión, de tipo mediterráneo y extravagante con un toque italiano.

Hakkasan

8 Hanway Place
London, W1T 1HB
Fitzrovia
Phone: +44 / 20 / 79 27 70 00
www.hakkasan.com

Opening hours: Restaurant: lunch Mon–Fri noon to 3 pm, Sat–Sun noon to 4.30 pm,
dinner Sun–Wed 6 pm to 11 pm, Thu–Sat 6 pm to midnight
Prices: £££
Cuisine: Chinese
Tube: Tottenham Court Road   **Map:** No. 5

Lydia Hearst's Special Tip
This dark, atmospheric Chinese restaurant is off the beaten track and the food is sublime.

The staging is exciting and unique: modern practicality is fused with traditional Chinese motifs. But the blend goes still further as the results obtained by an intelligent combination of excellent Far Eastern cuisine and Western experiences are fantastic. The Hakkasan on Hanway Place received its first Michelin star in 2003 and had already become one of the 50 best restaurants in the world by 2008.

Die Inszenierung ist aufregend und einzigartig: Moderne Sachlichkeit fusioniert mit traditionellen chinesischen Motiven. Aber die Verbindungen gehen noch weiter, denn die Ergebnisse, die eine exzellente fernöstliche Küche durch intelligente Kombination mit westlichen Erfahrungen hervorbringt, sind fantastisch. Wurde 2003 der erste Michelin-Stern errungen, gehört das Hakkasan am Hanway Place im Jahr 2008 schon zu den 50 besten Restaurants der Welt.

La mise en scène est à la fois captivante et unique : l'objectivité moderne fusionne avec des motifs chinois traditionnels. Mais les liens vont encore bien plus loin. En effet, les résultats d'une excellente cuisine de l'extrême orient combinée intelligemment aux expériences occidentales sont fantastiques. En 2003, le restaurant avait déjà obtenu la première étoile Michelin. Aujourd'hui, le Hakkasan au Hanway Place compte parmi les 50 meilleurs restaurants du monde entier !

La escenificación es excitante e incomparable: fusión del realismo moderno con motivos tradicionales chinos. Pero las combinaciones van todavía más lejos, pues los resultados que ofrece una excelente cocina del lejano oriente inteligentemente combinada con experiencias occidentales son fantásticos. En 2003 se obtuvo la primera estrella Michelin, considerándose al Hakkasan de la Hanway Place en el año 2008 como uno de los 50 mejores restaurantes del mundo.

Le Pain Quotidien

Royal Festival Hall
Belvedere Road
London, SE1 8XX
South Bank
Phone: +44 / 20 / 74 86 61 54
www.lepainquotidien.co.uk

Opening hours: Mon–Fri 7.30 am to 11 pm, Sat 9 am to 11 pm, Sun and public holiday 9 am to 10 pm
Prices: ££
Cuisine: French
Tube: Waterloo, Embankment, Charing Cross
Map: No. 6

The idea for this concept was conceived in the late eighties by Belgian chef Alain Coumont as he was dissatisfied with the quality of commercially available bread. He opened his first bakery in Brussels in 1990. Today, a top-quality range of bakery products and organic farm and garden produce is on offer. The atmosphere is authentic and inviting. A reflection on the simple things in life is the basis of his idea.

Die Idee zu diesem Konzept hatte Ende der 80er Jahre der belgische Chefkoch Alain Coumont, weil er mit der handelsüblichen Qualität des Brotes nicht zufrieden war. 1990 eröffnete er die erste eigene Bäckerei in Brüssel. Heute wird weltweit ein hochwertiger Mix aus Produkten der Backstube und ökologischem Feld- und Gartenbau geboten. Die Atmosphäre ist authentisch und einladend. Die Besinnung auf die einfachen Dinge des Lebens ist die Grundlage dieses Konzeptes.

A la fin des années 80, le chef de cuisine belge Alain Coumont a eu l'idée débouchant sur cette conception : il n'était pas satisfait de la qualité commerciale du pain habituelle. En 1990, il a ouvert la première boulangerie à son propre compte à Bruxelles. Aujourd'hui, on trouve, au Pain Quotidien un ensemble de produits de boulangerie mais aussi des fruits et légumes dont la production répond aux critères écologiques. L'atmosphère est authentique et accueillante. Les fondements d'une telle réussite ? Une réflexion sur les choses simples de la vie.

La idea de esta concepción la tuvo a finales de los años 80 el cocinero jefe belga Alain Coumont que no estaba en modo alguno contento con la calidad usual del pan. En 1990 abrió la primera panadería propia en Bruselas. Actualmente se ofrece a nivel mundial una valiosa mezcla de productos de panadería y productos ecológicos cultivados en campos y huertos. La atmósfera es auténtica y seductora. La base de su concepción la constituye el conocimiento de las cosas sencillas de la vida.

Pain d'épeautre au levain
Farine moulu sur pierre

1/1 £5,00
1/2 £2,40
1/4

Spelt sourdough
Stone ground flour

guette à l'ancienne
Façonnée à la main, fermentation lente, cuite sur pierre 1,50
Hand shaped, slowly fermented, baked on stone

ic Chocolate Bars
Milk / Dark

Mince Pies
Raisins, sultanas, currents,
apple, orange and lemon,
brandy, ginger, cinnamon,
butter, sugar, flour.

£4.00

Pecan Biscuits

Pecan Biscuits

Ginger Biscuits

Moro

34–36 Exmouth Market
London, EC1R 4QE
Islington
Phone: +44 / 20 / 78 33 83 36
www.moro.co.uk

Opening hours: Mon–Sat 12:30 pm to 2:30 pm, 7 pm to 10:30 pm
Prices: ££
Cuisine: Spanish, Moorish
Tube: Farringdon, Angel
Map: No. 7

The cuisine here is so unique that the guests' satisfaction has reached extraordinary dimensions; Moro in Clerkenwell is legendary. The secrets of Spanish cuisine are so well blended with Moorish-Oriental variations that the restaurant has already received numerous awards. Rectilinear wooden furniture characterises the warm atmosphere of the bright, spacious room which brings Mediterranean flair to London.

Hier wird so einzigartig gekocht, dass die Zufriedenheit der Gäste ungewöhnliche Ausmaße erreicht hat – Moro in Clerkenwell ist Kult. Die Geheimnisse der spanischen Küche werden mit maurisch-orientalischen Variationen vermischt, so gut, dass es schon mehrfach Auszeichnungen gab. Geradlinige Holzmöbel prägen die warme Atmosphäre des hellen, weiten Raums, der südländisches Flair nach London bringt.

Ici, la cuisine est si exceptionnelle que la satisfaction des clients atteint un niveau inaccoutumé – Moro à Clerkenwell est devenu un lieu culte du culinaire. Les secrets de la cuisine espagnole y sont si bien combinés aux variations mauresques et orientales que déjà plusieurs prix ont été décernés au restaurant. Des meubles de bois aux lignes claires structurent la salle vaste et lumineuse qui fait vivre à Londres des accents méditerranéens.

En este local se cocina de una forma tan singular que la satisfacción de los clientes alcanza cotas insólitas: Moro de Clerkenwell constituye un lugar de culto. Los secretos de la cocina española se mezclan con combinaciones orientales moriscas de una manera tan perfecta que se ha visto ya premiado en varias ocasiones. Unos muebles de madera de líneas rectas marcan la cálida atmósfera de un local amplio, luminoso, que ha acercado a Londres el ambiente de los países meridionales.

Nicole's

158 New Bond Street
London, W1S 2UB
Mayfair
Phone: +44 / 20 / 74 99 84 08
www.nicolefarhi.com

Opening hours: Mon–Sat 8.30 am to 6 pm
Prices: £££
Cuisine: Mediterranean, European
Tube: Piccadilly Circus, Oxford Circus, Bond Street, Green Park
Map: No. 8

Subtle elegance meets with serene tranquillity: this perfectly augments a lifestyle whose individuality bears the cosmopolitan hallmark of fashion designer Nicole Farhi. The creations fresh from the kitchen delight with this same sophistication. At Nicole's you also get the feeling of having found a place of peace in the hubbub of the metropolis.

Subtile Eleganz trifft auf heitere Gelassenheit – dies ist die perfekte Erweiterung einer Lifestyle-Welt, deren Individualität von der kosmopolitischen Handschrift der Modedesignerin Nicole Farhi geprägt wird. Mit eben solcher Raffinesse begeistern die frischen Kreationen der Küche. Dazu bekommt man im Nicole's das Gefühl, im Trubel der Weltstadt einen ruhigen Pol gefunden zu haben.

Une élégance subtile alliée à un flegme gai – telle est l'expression parfaite d'un mode de vie dont l'individualité porte la griffe cosmopolite de la créatrice de mode Nicole Farhi. Les créations culinaires, qui se recommandent par leur fraîcheur, enthousiasment par leur raffinement. Par ailleurs, on a l'impression dans le Nicole's d'avoir enfin trouvé un pôle de quiétude dans le tourbillon de cette ville cosmopolite.

Elegancia sutil junto a una calma serena constituye la ampliación perfecta de un mundo de estilo de vida cuya individualidad se halla marcada por la firma cosmopolita del diseñador de moda Nicole Farhi. Las creaciones de la cocina despiertan también entusiasmo con un refinamiento similar. Además se tiene la sensación, dentro del Nicole's, de haber encontrado un rincón de tranquilidad frente al ajetreo de esta ciudad mundial.

Nobu Berkeley ST

15 Berkeley Street
London, W1J 8DY
Fitzrovia
Phone: +44 / 20 / 72 90 92 22
www.noburestaurants.com

Opening hours: Restaurant: Mon–Fri lunch noon to 2.15 pm, Mon–Wed dinner 6 pm to 11 pm, Thu–Sat 6 pm to midnight, Thu–Sat dinner 6 pm to midnight, Sun 6 pm to 9.15 pm
Prices: £££
Cuisine: New style Japanese
Tube: Green Park   **Map:** No. 9

Lydia Hearst's Special Tip
All the hottest socials and stars can be spotted here. A "must have" is the signature black cod with miso.

Nobu Berkeley ST is one of the most elegant restaurants in London and has two stylish levels, each with a unique atmosphere. Specialities from a traditional Japanese wood-fired oven enhance the Nobu classics on the menu. Nobu Berkeley ST was awarded its first Michelin star in 2006, only five months after opening. This was followed in 2007 by the Top Newcomer Award. The city's most illustrious parties are celebrated here.

Nobu Berkeley ST verfügt als eines der elegantesten Restaurants Londons über zwei in ihrer Atmosphäre unverwechselbar stylishe Ebenen. Spezialitäten aus einem traditionellen japanischen Ofen, der mit Holz befeuert wird, bereichern die Nobu classics auf der Menükarte. Den ersten Michelin-Stern gewann Nobu Berkeley ST 2006 bereits fünf Monate nach der Eröffnung. 2007 folgte die Prämierung mit dem Top Newcomer Award. Die angesagtesten Partys der Stadt werden hier gefeiert.

Nobu Berkeley ST, un des restaurants les plus élégants de Londres, dispose de deux styles aux atmosphères originales. Des spécialités préparées à l'aide d'un four japonais traditionnel au bois enrichissent les Nobu classics sur la carte des menus. Nobu Berkeley ST a obtenu sa première étoile Michelin, dès 2006, alors qu'il venait à peine d'être ouvert depuis cinq mois. En 2007, il a reçu la distinction Top Newcomer Award. C'est dans ce restaurant que se déroulent les « partys » les plus en vue de la ville.

Nobu Berkeley ST cuenta, como uno de los restaurantes más elegantes de Londres, con dos plantas estilísticamente inconfundibles por lo que a su atmósfera se refiere. Unas especialidades que tienen su origen en una cocina tradicional japonesa que se alimenta con leña completan los Nobu classics en la carta de menús. Nobu Berkeley ST obtuvo la primera estrella Michelin en 2006, a los cinco meses tan solo de su apertura. En 2007 fue premiado con el Top Newcomer Award. Los Parties más famosos de la ciudad se celebran en este local.

Sake No Hana

23 St James's Street
London, SW1A 1HA
Westminster
Phone: +44 / 20 / 79 25 89 88
www.sakenohana.com

Opening hours: Lunch daily noon to 3 pm, dinner Mon–Sat 6 pm to midnight, Sun 6 pm to 11 pm
Prices: £££
Cuisine: Japanese, sushi
Tube: Green Park station
Map: No. 10

A Sake sommelier recommends a special drink to go with the delicious hari hari salad, taraba kani or buri nabe. Traditional Japanese sudare blinds at the large windows create completely inimitable light moods in the room – a room with an expensively designed timber framework of wood and bamboo on high walls that gives the impression of sitting in the shadows in a forest, with a gentle wind whistling through its branches. Japan in the middle of London.

Ein Sake-Sommelier empfiehlt ein spezielles Getränk zu köstlichem Hari Hari Salat, Taraba Kani oder Buri Nabe. Traditionelle japanische Sudare-Jalousien an den großen Fenstern erzeugen ganz einzigartige Lichtstimmungen im Raum, der mit aufwendig gestaltetem Fachwerk aus Holz und Bambus an hohen Wänden den Eindruck vermittelt, als säße man im Schatten eines Waldes, durch dessen Geäst eine leichte Brise weht. Japan mitten in London.

Un sommelier Sake recommande une boisson spéciale pour accompagner une salade Hari Hari, un crabe Taraba ou un Buri Nabe. Des jalousies japonaises traditionnelles Sudare devant de grandes fenêtres font naître une ambiance unique dans ce restaurant : des structures en bois et en bambous aux formes raffinées et des murs élevés donnent l'impression de se trouver dans l'ombre d'une forêt dont les branchages sont parcourus d'une légère brise. Le Japon en plein centre de Londres.

Un sumiller de sake le recomendará una bebida especial para acompañar la deliciosa ensalada Hari Hari, el Taraba Kani o el Buri Nabe. Unas tradicionales persianas japonesas Sudare colocadas en las amplias ventanas crean un ambiente de luz único dentro del local, y con su lujoso entramado de madera y bambú sobre unas paredes altas, transmiten la impresión de hallarse sentado entre las sombras de un bosque, a través de cuyo ramaje sopla una ligera brisa. Japón en el centro de Londres.

Salt Yard

54 Goodge Street
London, W1T 4NA
Camden
Phone: +44 / 20 / 76 37 06 57
www.saltyard.co.uk

Opening hours: Mon–Fri noon to 11 pm, Sat 5 pm to 11 pm
Prices: ££
Cuisine: Spanish & Italian
Tube: Tottenham Court Road, Oxford Circus, Goodge Street, Warren Street
Map: No. 11

Mediterranean spices fill the air of this restaurant with aromas. Thinly sliced Spanish chorizo or delicate ham from the Iberian Peninsula harmonise perfectly with a sherry, herb salami from Tuscany tastes excellent with a glass of prosecco. Here you can taste the difference between good and delectable. Tapas and cheese specialities complement the delicacies which are all traditionally produced.

Südländische Gewürze aromatisieren die Luft dieses Restaurants. Hauchzart geschnittene spanische Paprikawurst oder delikater Schinken der iberischen Halbinsel harmonieren perfekt mit einem Sherry, Kräutersalami aus der Toskana mundet exzellent zu einem Glas Prosecco. Hier schmeckt man den Unterschied zwischen gut und köstlich. Tapas und Käsespezialitäten ergänzen die Delikatessen, die alle aus traditioneller Herstellung stammen.

Des épices des pays du sud aromatisent l'air de ce restaurant. Le saucisson au poivron espagnol coupé fin ou un jambon délicieux provenant de la péninsule ibérique s'harmonise parfaitement avec un Sherry ; le saucisson aux herbes de la Toscane est du meilleur goût servi avec un verre de Prosecco. C'est ici que l'on peut sentir – jusqu'à en goûter la saveur – la différence existant entre bon et délicieux. Les tapas et les spécialités fromagères complètent des mets préparés selon les recettes traditionnelles.

Las especias de países meridionales impregnan de aroma el aire de este restaurante. El chorizo español cortado en finas rodajas o el delicado jamón procedente de la península ibérica armonizan perfectamente con un Sherry, y el salami o salchichón a las finas hierbas de Toscana se combina de manera excelente con un vaso de Prosecco. En este lugar se puede paladear y apreciar la diferencia que existe entre lo bueno y lo exquisito. Tapas y especialidades de quesos completan los manjares exquisitos que se caracterizan todos ellos por su origen tradicional.

St Alban

4–12 Lower Regent Street
London, SW1Y 4PE
St. James's
Phone: +44 / 20 / 74 99 85 58
www.stalban.net

Opening hours: Lunch Mon–Sat noon to 3 pm, dinner Mon–Sat 5.30 pm to midnight
Prices: £££
Cuisine: Modern Mediterranean
Tube: Piccadilly Circus
Map: No. 12

Lydia Hearst's Special Tip
With an extremely polite, welcoming staff, St. Alban is modern and chic with exquisite desserts.

Tranquillity and tension are combined in the trend-setting interior designed by Stiff & Trevillion, which provides the setting for this pearl of gastronomy. It is enhanced by decorations by Michael Craig-Martin and the painting "Jubilation" by Damien Hirst, which with its hundreds of butterfly wings symbolises beauty, love and fragility. Chris Corbin and Jeremy King expertly indulge their guests with a modern interpretation of Mediterranean cuisine.

Gelassenheit und Spannung verbindet das richtungsweisende Interieur von Stiff & Trevillion, das dieser gastronomischen Perle den Rahmen gibt. Bereichert wird es durch Dekorationen von Michael Craig-Martin und das Gemälde „Jubilation" von Damien Hirst, das mit hunderten Schmetterlingsflügeln Schönheit, Liebe und Zerbrechlichkeit symbolisiert. Chris Corbin und Jeremy King verwöhnen dazu gekonnt mit einer modern interpretierten mediterranen Küche.

L'intérieur de Stiff & Trevillion crée des perspectives en alliant le flegme au suspens et fournit ainsi le cadre de cette perle de la gastronomie. Cet intérieur est encore rehaussé par des décorations de Michael Craig-Martin et le tableau « Jubilation » de Damien Hirst qui, à partir de centaines d'ailes de papillons, symbolise la beauté, l'amour ainsi que leur fragilité et évanescent. Par ailleurs, Chris Corbin et Jeremy King savent choyer leurs clients par une interprétation moderne de la cuisine méditerranéenne.

El interior con visión de futuro de Stiff & Trevillion, que constituye el marco de esta perla gastronómica, combina placidez y suspense. Se halla enriquecido con decoraciones de Michael Craig-Martin y el cuadro "Jubilation" de Damien Hirst que simboliza, con cientos de alas de mariposas, la belleza, el amor y la fragilidad. Chris Corbin y Jeremy King agasajan además a los clientes de forma magistral con una cocina mediterránea de acuerdo con una interpretación moderna.

The Zetter Restaurant

St. John's Square
86–88 Clerkenwell Road
London, EC1M 5RJ
Clerkenwell
Phone: +44 / 20 / 73 24 44 55
www.thezetter.com

Opening hours: Breakfast Mon–Fri 7 am to 10.30 am, Sat+Sun 7.30 am to 11 am,
brunch 11 am to 3 pm, Sun 11 am to 4 pm, lunch Mon–Fri noon to 2.30 pm,
dinner Thu–Sat 6 pm to 11 pm, Sun–Wed 6 pm to 10.30 pm
Prices: ££
Cuisine: Seasonal, clean-flavoured, modern Mediterranean food
Tube: Farringdon
Map: No. 13

The converted Zetter Building, a 19th-century warehouse, today houses a city hotel with style and
unique charm. Located between the East and the West End, the restaurant offers modern Mediterranean dishes – always freshly made. Large windows let in life on the street as if you were sitting at the
tables on St. John's Square. In the summer there is scarcely a better place for a cosy weekend brunch.

Das umgebaute Zetter-Building, ein ehemaliges Lagerhaus aus dem 19. Jahrhundert, beherbergt heute
ein Hotel mit Stil und individuellem Charme. Zwischen East und West End gelegen, offeriert das Restaurant modern-mediterrane Speisen – immer frisch hergestellt. Große Fenster lassen das Leben von
der Straße herein, als säße man an den Tischen am St. John's Square – im Sommer gibt es kaum
einen besseren Platz für einen gemütlichen Wochenendbrunch.

Le bâtiment Zetter, un ancien entrepôt du 19ième siècle, abrite aujourd'hui un restaurant d'un style et
d'un charme individuel. Situé entre East et West End, ce restaurant offre des repas méditerranéens modernes – préparés à partir des meilleurs ingrédients qui se recommandent par leur fraîcheur. De grandes
fenêtres laissent la vie de la rue pénétrer à l'intérieur comme si l'on se trouvait à une table du St. John's
Square. En été, on trouverait difficilement un meilleur endroit pour un brunch agréable de fin de semaine.

El remodelado Zetter-Building, que era anteriormente un almacén del siglo XIX, cobija en la actualidad
a un hostal urbano con estilo y encanto individual. Situado entre el East y el West End, ofrece el restaurante platos mediterráneos modernos, preparados siempre en el momento. Unas amplias ventanas
dejan que la vida de la calle penetre en el local como si uno estuviera sentado en las mesas colocadas
en St. John's Square; en verano apenas existe un lugar mejor para un Brunch agradable de fin de
semana.

Tom's Delicatessen

226 Westbourne Grove
London, W11 2RH
Notting Hill
Phone: +44 / 20 / 72 21 88 18
www.tomconranrestaurants.co.uk

Opening hours: Mon–Sat 8 am to 6.30 pm, Sun 9 am to 6.30 pm
Prices: £
Cuisine: Modern English, delicatessen
Tube: Notting Hill Gate
Map: No. 14

Lydia Hearst's Special Tip
This is a local favorite! It is a relatively bijoux cafe with an excellent and cheerful staff and delicious food.

Tom Conran's combination of café and deli in Notting Hill embodies the new style of presenting and enjoying fine foods and wines. While eating at a table the eyes wander over a choice selection of various foods. Comfortable hospitality without culinary compromise. Artists and business people, successful singles and rushed mothers – all of them feel attracted to the fine delicacies.

Tom Conran's Kombination aus Café und Feinkostgeschäft in Notting Hill verkörpert den neuen Stil in der Präsentation und im Genuss feiner Lebensmittel und Weine. Während des Speisens am Tisch spazieren die Augen über ein erlesenes und vielfältiges Angebot. Behagliche Gastlichkeit ohne kulinarische Kompromisse. Künstler und Geschäftsleute, erfolgreiche Singles und eilige Mütter – alle fühlen sich von den feinen Köstlichkeiten angezogen.

La combinaison d'un café et d'une épicerie fine de Tom Conran à Notting Hill incarne le nouveau style qui prévaut pour la présentation et la délectation de vins et de produits d'épicerie fine. Une gamme variée et savamment recherchée de produits s'offre aux regards de ceux qui prennent leur repas aux différentes tables. Une hospitalité empreinte de confort sans compromis culinaire. De tels délices exercent leurs attraits sur tous – qu'il s'agisse de mères pressées, de personnes venant des milieux artistiques ou d'affaires, de couples soucieux de leur intimité ou de célibataires portés par le succès.

La combinación de Café y tienda de comestibles finos de Tom Conran en Notting Hill encarna el nuevo estilo en la presentación y el disfrute de vino y productos alimenticios finos. Mientras se está sentado a la mesa durante la comida se pasea la vista por toda una oferta de productos variados y selectos. Hospitalidad agradable sin compromisos culinarios. Artistas y hombres de negocios, Singles que han obtenido éxito y madres con prisas: todos se sienten atraídos por las finas exquisiteces que se ofrecen.

Wahaca

66 Chandos Place
London, WC2N 4HG
Covent Garden
Phone: +44 / 20 / 72 40 18 83
www.wahaca.co.uk

Opening hours: Mon–Sat noon to 11 pm, Sun noon to 10.30 pm
Prices: £
Cuisine: Mexican
Tube: Charing Cross, Covent Garden, Embankment, Leicester Square
Map: No.15

Tomatillo-coloured lamps, wooden crates full of fruits, chilli plants in buckets and many other market colours and paraphernalia radiate an infectious sense of happiness. The guests enter the Wahaca in serpentine queues. But it's worth the wait: enchiladas, tostadas, tacos and quesadillas. Pungent and/or fruity, the apparently endless choice of genuine Mexican delicacies is as colourful as the restaurant.

Tomatillofarbene Lampen, Holzkisten voller Früchte, Chilipflanzen in Kübeln und viele andere Markt-farben und Utensilien versprühen eine ansteckende Fröhlichkeit. In langen Reihen schlängeln sich die Gäste ins Wahace. Doch das Warten lohnt sich: Enchiladas, Tostadas, Tacos und Quesadillas – scharf und/oder fruchtig: so farbenfroh wie das Restaurant präsentiert sich auch die endlos scheinende Aus-wahl echter mexikanischer Delikatessen.

Des lampes couleur de « tomatille », des caisses de bois remplies de fruits, des plantes de « chiles » dans des jardinières et bien d'autres couleurs et ustensiles typiques pour les marchés de l'Amérique du Sud font naître une gaîté communicative. Les clients font la queue en longues files. Mais une telle attente est récompensée : Enchiladas, Tostadas, Tacos et Quesadillas – épicés et/ou fruités : le choix apparemment presque infini des mets mexicains originaux regorge tout autant de couleurs que le restaurant lui-même.

Lámpara de color tomatillo, cajas de madera llenas de frutas, macetas con plantas de Chili y muchos otros colores del mercado y utensilios transmiten una alegría contagiosa. Los clientes esperan guar-dando largas colas en el Wahace. Pero la espera merece la pena: Enchiladas, Tostadas, Tacos y Que-sadillas – picantes y/o afrutadas: con el mismo colorido alegre que el restaurante se presenta también el surtido aparentemente interminable de verdaderas Delikatessen mejicanas.

CLUBS, LOUNGES & BARS

1707 Wine Bar

181 Piccadilly
London, W1A 1ER
Westminster
Phone: +44 / 20 / 77 34 80 40
www.fortnumandmason.com

Opening hours: Mon–Sat noon to 11 pm, Sun noon to 5.30 pm
Prices: £££
Tube: Green Park, Piccadilly
Map: No. 16

The name of the Wine Bar designed by David Collins is a proud reference to the year in which Fortnum & Mason was established. In this successful combination of tradition and modernity right next to the Fresh Food Hall in Piccadilly the journey to the "good old days" begins. A wide selection of exquisite and rare wines and champagnes accompanies delicious menus which chef de cuisine Shaun Hill creates from fresh ingredients directly from the Food Hall.

Der Name der von David Collins designten Wine Bar weist stolz auf das Jahr hin, in dem Fortnum & Mason gegründet wurde. Gleich neben der Fresh Food Hall am Piccadilly beginnt hier in einer gelungenen Verbindung von Tradition und Moderne die Reise in die „gute alte Zeit". Eine große Auswahl exquisiter und seltener Weine und Champagner begleitet delikate Menüs, die Küchenchef Shaun Hill mit frischen Zutaten direkt aus der Food Hall kreiert.

Le nom du Wine Bar conçu par David Collins rappelle fièrement l'année à laquelle Fortnum & Mason a été créé. Tout à côté du Fresh Food Hall à Piccadilly commence le voyage dans le « bon vieux temps » qui devient possible grâce à cette association réussie de la tradition et de la modernité. Une sélection étendue d'excellents vins et de champagnes rares accompagne des menus délicats que le chef de cuisine Shaun Hill crée à partir d'aliments frais provenant directement du Food Hall.

El nombre de Wine Bar con el que ha sido bautizado por David Collins hace orgullosamente referencia al año en el que se fundó el Fortnum & Mason. Justo al lado del Fresh Food Hall en Piccadilly comienza, en esta acertada combinación de tradición y modernidad, el viaje a los "buenos tiempos antiguos". Un gran surtido de vinos y champanes exquisitos y poco frecuentes acompaña a unos menús delicados creados por el jefe de cocina, Shaun Hill, con ingredientes frescos que llegan directamente del Food Hall.

Adventure Bar & Lounge

91a Battersea Rise
London, SW11 1HW
Wandsworth
Phone: +44 / 20 / 72 23 17 00
www.adventurebar.co.uk

Opening hours: Sun–Thu 5 pm to midnight, Fri+Sat 5 pm to 2 am
Prices: ££
Tube: Clapham South
Map: No. 17

Thirsty night-time revellers are drawn to the vibrant centre of Clapham where the Battersea Adventure Club is located. Although not very large, it impresses with its electrifying atmosphere full of fun and entertainment. The cocktails are first-class and in combination with excellent service the night turns effortlessly to day here.

Durstige Nachtschwärmer zieht es in die lebhafte Mitte Claphams, denn hier liegt der Battersea Adventure Club. Obwohl nicht allzu groß, besticht er durch seine elektrisierende Atmosphäre voller Spaß und Unterhaltung. Die Cocktails sind erstklassig und in Kombination mit einem hervorragenden Service wird hier die Nacht mühelos zum Tag.

Les noctambules qui désirent boire quelque chose sont attirés par le centre vivant de Clapham où se trouve le Battersea Adventure Club. Bien qu'il ne soit pas trop grand, il séduit par son atmosphère électrisante et divertissante. Les cocktails, de premier choix sont combinés à un excellent service de sorte que l'on peut « faire de la nuit le jour » sans aucun problème.

Los noctámbulos sedientos acuden al centro animado de Clapham, pues es aquí donde se encuentra el Battersea Adventure Club. A pesar de no ser muy grande, seduce por su electrizante atmósfera llena de distracción y entretenimiento. Los Cocktails son de primera clase y combinados con un excelente servicio hacen que la noche transcurra sin enterarse hasta el amanecer.

Artesian Bar

The Langham
1c Portland Place, Regent Street
London, W1B 1JA
Westminster
Phone: +44 / 20 / 76 36 10 00
www.artesian-bar.co.uk

Opening hours: Daily 10.30 am to midnight
Prices: ££
Tube: Bond Street, Oxford Circus
Map: No. 18

Russell James' Special Tip

With painterly grace, barkeeps at the glamorous Langham Hotel lounge shake and stir winning drinks.

A refreshing lightness is exuded by the traditional elements which David Collins Studio has transferred here with bold momentum into the 21st century: crowned with silver-leaf bevelled mirrors and sparkling chandeliers and brought back to earth by mulberry-coloured accents. This fascinating blend caused professionals to invent the term "Chinese Chippendale" style.

Erfrischende Leichtigkeit geht von den traditionellen Elementen aus, die hier vom David Collins Studio mit kühnem Schwung ins 21. Jahrhundert transferiert, mit geschliffenen Silberspiegeln und glitzernden Lüstern gekrönt und durch maulbeerfarbene Akzente wieder geerdet werden. Für diese Verschmelzung zu einem faszinierenden Ensemble fand die Fachwelt den Begriff „Chinese Chippendale Style".

Les éléments traditionnels catapultés ici audacieusement par le David Collins Studio en plein 21ième siècle tels que des miroirs d'argent biseautés couronnés par des lustres brillants créent une légèreté presque aérienne que des accents de la couleur framboise rattachent au réel. Les spécialistes ont créé la notion de « Chinese Chippendale Style » pour cette fusion qui réalise une synthèse de styles aussi fascinante.

Ligereza refrescante procedente de los elementos tradicionales que se han visto transferidos aquí por David Collins Studio con un atrevido impulso hasta el siglo 21, coronados por unos espejos de plata biselados y por unas arañas destellantes, y que conectan de nuevo con la realidad a través de unos toques de color morado. Para esta fusión en un conjunto fascinante han encontrado los expertos la denominación de estilo "Chinese Chippendale".

Buddha Bar

8 Victoria Embankment
London, WC2R 2AB
Covent Garden
Phone: +44 / 20 / 33 71 77 77
www.buddhabar-london.com

Opening hours: Mon–Fri noon until open end, Sat 4 pm until open end
Prices: ££
Cuisine: Contemporary Pan-Asian
Tube: Covent Garden
Map: No. 19

Lighting, furnishings and lounge music create a harmonious chilled-out atmosphere in this mega-location dominated by a huge statue of Buddha. This is where the city's movers and shakers come as well as an international clientele who is cosmopolitan and trend-conscious, and enjoys the relaxed feeling on which the concept is based by founder Raymond Visan from Paris. Since 1999 the Buddha Bar feeling for home has been available on CD, too.

Licht, Einrichtung und Loungemusik erzeugen eine stimmige Chillout-Atmosphäre in dieser von einer riesigen Buddhastatue beherrschten Megalocation. Hierher kommen die Movers und Shakers der Stadt sowie ein internationales Publikum, das weltoffen und trendbewusst ist und das entspannte Gefühl mag, auf dem das Konzept des Gründers Raymond Visan aus Paris basiert. Das Buddha Bar-Feeling für zu Hause gibt es seit 1999 auch auf CD.

La lumière, l'ameublement et la musique de salon créent une atmosphère relaxante dans ce grand local que domine une statue géante de Buddha. C'est ici que viennent les « movers » et les « shakers » de la ville ainsi qu'un public international ouvert au monde et conscient des tendances du moment. Ils apprécient le climat décontracté sur lequel repose la conception du fondateur, Raymond Visan de Paris. Depuis 1999, un CD permet de recréer chez soi le « feeling » du Buddha Bar.

La luz, la decoración y la música de Lounge crean una armoniosa atmósfera Chillout dentro de este inmenso local presidido por una gigantesca estatua de Buda. A este local acuden los Movers y Shakers de la ciudad así como un público internacional cosmopolita y moderno, y que disfruta con la sensación relajada sobre la que se basa la concepción del fundador Raymond Visan de París. El Buddha Bar-Feeling para el propio hogar se halla también disponible desde 1999 en un CD.

Ghost Inc

7–11 Queensberry Place
London, SW7 2DL
Kensington
Phone: +44 / 20 / 75 89 89 79
www.ghostbar.co.uk

Opening hours: Tue–Sun 5.30 pm to 2.30 am
Prices: ££
Tube: South Kensington
Map: No. 20

Gleaming mirrors and black leather upholstery form the counterpoint to bold graffiti which designer Robbie Clydesdale created in Ghost Inc. in collaboration with numerous street artists. This dramatic background underlines the club character of the cocktail bar where celebrities of the international music and fashion scene who travel between Miami and Moscow for their fashionable gigs celebrate parties and individuality.

Schimmernde Spiegel und schwarze Lederpolsterungen sind der Kontrapunkt zu kühnen Graffitis, die der Designer Robbie Clydesdale zusammen mit vielen Straßenkünstlern im Ghost Inc. schuf. Diese dramatische Inszenierung unterstreicht den Clubcharakter der Cocktailbar, in der Größen der internationalen Musik- und Fashionszene, die für ihre angesagten Gigs zwischen Miami und Moskau unterwegs sind, Partys und Individualität zelebrieren.

Des miroirs reluisants et des capitonnages en cuir noir font effet de contraste face à des graffitis audacieux créés dans le Ghost Inc. par le designer Robbie Clydesdale en collaboration avec de nombreux artistes de rue. Cette mise en scène dramatique souligne le caractère de club de ce bar de cocktails. Des célébrités internationales des milieux de la mode et de la musique, de passage entre Miami et Moscou pour leurs numéros en vogue, y organisent des « partys » et mettent en scène leur individualité.

Unos espejos resplandecientes y unos tapizados de cuero de color negro constituyen el contrapunto a unos atrevidos grafitis creados por el diseñador Robbie Clydesdale junto con muchos artistas callejeros en Ghost Inc. Esta dramática escenificación subraya el carácter de Club del Cocktailbar, en el que han celebrado Partys y actos individuales grandes personajes del mundo de la música y de la moda que se han desplazado entre Miami y Moscú para acudir a actos comprometidos.

Mamounia Lounge

37a Curzon Street
London, W1J 7TX
Westminster
Phone: +44 / 20 / 76 29 22 11
www.mamounialounge.com

Opening hours: Open throughout the day
Prices: ££
Tube: Green Park
Map: No. 21

Lydia Hearst's Special Tip
The place to go if you're looking to unwind; elegant, chic and surrounded by Moroccan art and artistic people.

London or Morocco? Incense, rhythmic pulsating sound and a sumptuous décor captivate the senses. This luxurious symbiosis of elegance, glamour and comfort creates an oasis whose opulent atmosphere conjures up expectations which are met by the outstanding specialities of Moroccan, Lebanese and Mediterranean cuisines. The Arabian Nights experience is rounded off by enjoying a water pipe.

London oder Marokko? Weihrauch, rhythmisch pulsierende Klänge und eine kostbare Ausstattung umfangen die Sinne. Der Luxus dieser Symbiose aus Eleganz, Glamour und Bequemlichkeit schafft eine Oase, deren opulente Atmosphäre Erwartungen heraufbeschwört, welche die hervorragenden Spezialitäten der marokkanisch-libanesisch-mediterranen Küche erfüllen. Der Genuss einer Wasserpfeife rundet das Erlebnis von Tausendundeiner Nacht ab.

Londres ou le Maroc? De l'encens, des sons, des pulsations rythmées et un ameublement raffiné accueillent les sens. L'impression de luxe qui naît de cette symbiose entre l'élégance, le glamour et le confort crée une oasis dont l'atmosphère opulente suscitent des désirs que comblent les excellentes spécialités d'une cuisine méditerranéenne influencée ici par le Maroc et le Liban. Les plaisirs du narguilé complètent une expérience qui nous conduit tout droit au pays des mille et une nuits.

¿Londres o Marruecos? Los sentidos quedan atrapados entre el incienso, unos sonidos rítmicos y una lujosa decoración. El lujo de esta simbiosis de elegancia, glamour y comodidad crea un oasis cuya opulenta atmósfera suscita unas expectativas que se ven cumplidas por las extraordinarias especialidades de la cocina marroquí-libanesa-mediterránea. El placer de una pipa de agua redondea la aventura de mil y una noches.

The Loft

67 Clapham High Street
London, SW4 7TG
Lambeth
Phone: +44 / 20 / 76 27 07 92
www.theloft-clapham.co.uk

Opening hours: Mon–Thu 6 pm to midnight, Fri 5 pm to 1.30 am, Sat noon to 1.30 am,
Sun noon to midnight
Prices: ££
Tube: Clapham North
Map: No. 22

Russell James' Special Tip
Industrially cool and impeccably stylish, this lounge serves cocktails crafted with house-infused ingredients.

With a view of the hustle and bustle of Clapham High Street, sophisticated dinners inspired by modern European cuisine are served. Combined with the lascivious charm of a bar, The Loft expertly transports guests away from the busyness of the world. *Time Out* recently voted it best bar in the city because of its excellent cocktails and its large choice of international beers.

Mit dem Ausblick auf das Gedränge und die lärmende Geschäftigkeit der Hauptstraße Claphams werden hier anspruchsvolle, von der modernen europäischen Küche inspirierte Dinner serviert. Kombiniert mit dem lasziven Charme einer Bar, entrückt The Loft den Gast gekonnt dem Treiben der Welt. Jüngst wurde es wegen seiner ausgezeichneten Cocktails sowie einer großen Auswahl internationaler Biere durch *Time Out* zur besten Bar der Stadt gewählt.

En jouissant d'un point de vue sur la cohue et l'activité bruyante propre à la rue principale de Clapham, on peut se faire servir des dîners inspirés par une cuisine européenne moderne de la meilleure qualité. Grâce à ces délices culinaires combinés aux charmes lascifs d'un bar, The Loft soustrait, avec brio, les visiteurs aux agitations de ce monde. En raison de l'excellence de ses cocktails ainsi que de son choix très étendu de bières internationales, il a été désigné comme le meilleur bar de la ville par *Time Out*.

Con la vista del gentío y de la febril actividad comercial que se desarrolla en la calle principal de Clapham, se puede disfrutar en este local de almuerzos exquisitos inspirados en la moderna cocina europea. Combinado con el lascivo encanto de un Bar, sustrae conscientemente The Loft al cliente del bullicio del mundo exterior. Recientemente ha sido elegido por *Time Out* como el mejor Bar de la ciudad debido a sus extraordinarios Cocktails así como a una gran selección internacional de cervezas.

Westbourne House

65 Westbourne Grove
London, W2 4UJ
Westminster
Phone: +44 / 20 / 72 29 22 33
www.westbournehouse.net

Opening hours: Daily 11 am to midnight
Prices: £££
Tube: Bayswater
Map: No. 23

Lydia Hearst's Special Tip
Extremely elegant with a contemporary yet sophisticated vibe, this is one of the trendiest places in London.

"What cocktails will not cure, there is no cure for." Under this motto, the subtle mixture of Parisian boutique and Manhattan loft brought a touch of elegance, both optically and acoustically, to the heart of
Westbourne Grove in 2007. Contrast and complementation are on the programme here: a quick lunch
or a leisurely brunch, brief encounters or protracted hedonistic stays.

„Was Cocktails nicht heilen, ist nicht heilbar." Mit diesem Motto brachte die raffinierte Mixtur aus Pari-
ser Boutique und Manhattan Loft 2007 einen Touch von Eleganz in das Herz von Westbourne
Grove – sowohl optisch als auch akustisch. Kontrast und Ergänzung sind hier Programm – schneller
Lunch oder ausgedehnter Brunch, kurze Treffen oder schier endlose, genussreiche Aufenthalte.

« Ce que les cocktails ne peuvent pas guérir, est inguérissable. » Fidèle à cette devise, ce mélange raffiné de boutique parisienne et de Manhattan Loft a amené, en 2007 une note d'élégance au cœur de
Westbourne Grove – aussi bien sur le plan optique qu'acoustique. Les contrastes et les compléments
font ici naturellement parti du programme – qu'il s'agisse de lunchs rapides ou de brunchs prolongés,
de courtes entrevues ou de rencontres sans fin sous le signe des plaisirs épicuriens.

"Lo que no se cure con Cocktails, no tiene curación posible." Con este lema ha introducido la refinada
mezcla entre una boutique parisina y un Loft de Manhattan 2007 un toque de elegancia en el corazón
de Westbourne Grove – tanto desde un punto de vista óptico como acústico. Contrastes y complemen-
tos constituyen aquí el programa; un Lunch rápido o un Brunch reposado, unos encuentros breves o
permanencias deliciosas, prácticamente interminables.

SHOPS

Bamford & Sons

The Old Bank
31 Sloane Square
Kensington
London, SW1W 8AQ
Phone: +44 / 20 / 78 81 80 10
www.bamfordwayoflife.com

Opening hours: Mon–Tue, Thu–Sat 9.30 am to 6 pm, Wed 9.30 am to 7 pm, Sun noon to 5 pm
Products: Organic luxury; natural dyed cashmere, men's, women's, bath and body, baby, watches, gadgets and books
Tube: Sloane Square, Knightsbridge
Map: No. 24

The Bamford Collections encompasses internationally renowned men's and women's ready-to-wear, accessories, home and lifestyle products as well as a bath and body collection. Within the ready-to-wear collections only natural materials are used and organic fabrics are integrated wherever possible.

Die Bamford Collections umfassen international bekannte Herren- und Damenkonfektionsbekleidung, Accessoires, Wohn- und Lifestyle-Produkte sowie eine Bade- und Körperpflegeserie. Für die Konfektionsbekleidung werden ausschließlich natürliche Materialien verwendet und ökologische Textilien integriert, wo immer dies möglich ist.

Les collections Bamford s'étendent des vêtements de confection pour femmes et hommes internationalement connus aux accessoires et aux produits destinés à l'habitat et au Lifestyle. Elles englobent aussi une série de produits cosmétiques et de soins corporels. Seulement des matériaux naturels et des textiles écologiques sont utilisés pour les vêtements de confection chaque fois que cela est possible.

Las Bamford Collections comprenden ropa de confección internacionalmente conocida de damas y caballeros, accesorios, productos para el hogar y productos Lifestyle, así como una serie de productos de baño y para el cuidado corporal. Para la ropa de confección se utilizan exclusivamente materiales naturales y tejidos ecológicos, siempre que ello resulta factible.

Borough Market

8 Southwark Sreet
London, SE1 1TL
Southwark
Phone: +44 / 20 / 74 07 10 02
www.boroughmarket.org.uk

Opening hours: Thu 11 am to 5 pm, Fri noon to 6 pm, Sat 9 am to 4 pm
Products: Delicatessen from all around the world, vegetables and fruits
Tube: London Bridge
Map: No. 25

Russell James' Special Tip
Find farm-fresh produce, artisanal cheeses and other delights at this maze-like market near London Bridge.

The city's oldest market is located on the South Bank of the Thames. It has its roots in Roman times, but was established at its present location in the mid-eighteenth century. Its living scenery is known worldwide as the backdrop of many films. Nowadays, wholesalers bustle around here from two at night. Then in the morning, the Londoners come, even from more distant parts of the city, to buy their fruit, vegetables, meat, or bread.

Der älteste Markt der Stadt befindet sich am Südufer der Themse. Er führt seine Wurzeln in die römische Zeit zurück, erhielt seinen heutigen Standort jedoch Mitte des 18. Jahrhunderts. Seine lebendige Szenerie wurde weltweit als Kulisse vieler Spielfilme bekannt. Heutzutage tummeln sich Großhändler hier schon ab zwei Uhr nachts. Am Morgen kommen dann die Londoner – auch aus entfernteren Stadtteilen – um ihr Obst, Gemüse, Fleisch oder Brot einzukaufen.

Le plus ancien marché de la ville se trouve sur la rive sud de la Tamise. Ses origines remontent jusqu'à l'époque romaine, toutefois son emplacement actuel date du milieu du 18ème siècle. Son décor vivant est connu dans le monde entier comme coulisse d'un grand nombre de films. Aujourd'hui les grossistes travaillent ici, au milieu de la nuit, dès deux heures du matin. Le matin, les londoniens eux-mêmes affluent – même des quartiers les plus éloignés – pour acheter leurs fruits, leurs viandes ou leur pain.

El mercado más antiguo de la ciudad se encuentra en la ribera sur del Támesis. Hunde sus raíces en la época romana, aunque su actual ubicación no se fijó hasta mediados del siglo XVIII. Su escenario rebosante de vida se conoce en todo el mundo por haber sido utilizado como decorado de numerosas películas. Actualmente corretean ya por él los mayoristas a partir de las dos de la madrugada. Posteriormente acudirán los londinenses por la mañana, incluso desde los barrios más lejanos de la ciudad, para comprar frutas, verduras, carnes o pan.

THE MARKET PORTER
FINE WINES
Continental Lagers
TRADITIONAL
CONFIT DE CANARD
CONFIT D'OIE
CUISSE
RASTEAU
FRAGILE

Maria's Market Café

MARIA'S MARKET CAFE

SPECIAL

BACON CHEESE
AND BUBBLE BAP

FARMER SHARP'S
GALLOWAY STEAK BAP
WITH ROCKET SALAD £3·00
WITH ONIONS OR
MUSHROOMS £3·50

Camden Market

Camden High Street and side streets
London
Camden Town
www.camdenlock.net

Opening hours: Daily
Products: Clothing, shoes, jewelry, arts and craft, gifts
Tube: Camden Town, Chalk Farm
Map: No. 26

The heart of Camden Market is Camden Lock Market, which opened in the mid-1970s. Most of the stalls with merchandise like jewelry, vintage fashion, furniture, and all kinds of odds and ends are in one hall. More markets have been added since then. The area is considered a great place for musicians to play.

Das Herz von Camden Market ist der Mitte der 70er-Jahre eröffnete Camden Lock Market. Die meisten der Buden mit zum Beispiel Schmuck, Vintage-Mode oder Möbeln und jeder Menge Krimskrams befinden sich in einer Halle. Seit den Anfängen sind nach und nach weitere Märkte hinzugekommen. Das Areal gilt als Tummelplatz für Musiker.

Le coeur de Camden Market est le Camden Lock Market, ouvert au milieu des années 70. La plupart des stands avec de la bijouterie, de la mode Vintage, des meubles et des objets divers se trouvent dans une salle. Depuis cette époque, plusieurs marchés s'y sont ajoutés. Le quartier est connu comme un lieu de rencontre des musiciens.

El corazón del mercado es el Camden Lock Market, inaugurado a mediados de los años 70. La mayoría de los puestos que venden joyas, moda vintage, muebles y toda clase de trastos se encuentran en un mismo pabellón. Desde sus comienzos se han ido uniendo otros mercadillos a esta zona, frecuentada también por músicos callejeros.

Coco de Mer

23 Monmouth Street
London, WC2H 9DD
Covent Garden
Phone: +44 / 20 / 78 36 88 82
www.coco-de-mer.com

Opening hours: Mon–Sat 11 am to 7 pm, Thu to 8 pm, Sun noon to 6 pm
Products: Lingerie, erotic literature, tools for bedroom art, massage oils
Tube: Covent Garden, Leicester Square, Tottenham Court Road
Map: No. 27

Erotic luxury in a class of its own – in the high-class atmosphere of this quite exceptional sex shop you can discover erotic accessories which have only one purpose: to awaken sensual fantasies. The shop is named after the very rare and thus costly fruit of the Seychelle palm, the shape of which is reminiscent of female buttocks. Here both men and women find everything for thrilling hours *à deux*.

Erotischer Luxus der Extraklasse – in diesem ganz besonderen Sexshop kann man in edlem Ambiente erotische Accessoires entdecken, die nur eine Aufgabe haben: sinnliche Fantasien zu wecken. Namensgeberin ist die sehr seltene und daher wertvolle Frucht der Seychellenpalme, deren Form an einen weiblichen Po erinnert. Männer wie Frauen finden hier alles für prickelnde Stunden zu zweit.

Un luxe érotique de première classe – dans ce sex-shop tout particulier on peut découvrir des accessoires érotiques de haut de gamme dans une ambiance noble qui n'ont qu'un seul but : éveiller l'imagination sensuelle. Le fruit du palmier des Seychelles très rare et, de ce fait, très précieux possède une forme qui évoque le bas du dos féminin. C'est pourquoi il a été choisi comme nom de ce magasin. Les hommes tout aussi bien que les femmes trouvent ici tout ce dont ils ont besoin pour des heures excitantes à deux.

Lujo erótico de clase extra; en este Sexshop de tipo realmente especial se pueden encontrar, dentro de un ambiente agradable, accesorios eróticos que solamente pretenden servir para un objetivo: despertar fantasías sensuales. Su nombre recuerda a un exquisito y raro fruto de la palma de las Seychelles cuya forma recuerda al trasero femenino. Tanto los hombres como las mujeres pueden encontrar aquí todo lo necesario para unas horas picantes.

Covent Garden

Covent Garden
London
www.coventgardenmarket.co.uk

Opening hours: Daily 10 am to 8 pm
Products: Fashion, womenswear and menswear, shoes, gifts, jewelry, arts and crafts and lots more
Tube: Covent Garden, Leicester Square, Charing Cross
Map: No. 28

Here you find everything that the heart desires. Covent Garden, formerly a fruit, vegetable and flower market, is today the vital heart of a quarter with numerous public cultural events, a wealth of shops, boutiques, theatres, cinemas, galleries, restaurants, cafés, and bars. And twice a week, artists and farmers bring their handiwork and fresh produce to the original Farmers' Market.

Hier findet man alles, was das Herz begehrt. Covent Garden – früher ein Markt für Obst, Gemüse, und Blumen – ist heute der lebendige Mittelpunkt eines Viertels mit zahlreichen öffentlichen kulturellen Veranstaltungen, einer Fülle von Läden, Boutiquen, Theater, Kinos, Galerien, Restaurants, Cafés und Bars. Und zweimal in der Woche bringen Künstler und Landwirte ihre handwerklichen Erzeugnisse und frischen Lebensmittel zum original Farmers' Market.

On trouve ici tout ce qui tient à cœur. Covent Garden – dans le passé, un marché pour les fruits, les légumes et les fleurs – est devenu aujourd'hui le centre d'un quartier offrant une multitude de manifestations culturelles publiques, une abondance de magasins, de boutiques, de théâtres, de cinémas, de galeries et de restaurants, de cafés et de bars. Et, deux fois par semaine, les artistes et les agriculteurs amènent leurs produits artisanaux et leurs produits alimentaires frais au Farmers' Market original.

Aquí puede encontrar uno todo lo que desee. Covent Garden, antiguamente un mercado de frutas, hortalizas y flores, constituye actualmente el centro lleno de vida de un barrio con múltiples actos culturales y públicos, con una gran cantidad de tiendas, boutiques, teatros, cines, galerías, restaurantes, cafés y bares. Y dos días de la semana traen los artistas y los agricultores sus obras de artesanía y sus productos alimenticios frescos al Farmers' Market original.

Daunt Books

83 Marylebone High Street
London, W1U 4QW
Marylebone
Phone: +44 / 20 / 72 24 22 95
www.dauntbooks.co.uk

Opening hours: Mon–Sat 9 am to 7.30 pm, Sun 11 am to 6 pm
Products: Travel guides and novels arranged by country, secondhand literature, children's books, books on cookery and interior design
Tube: Baker Street, Regent's Park
Map: No. 29

The city's finest bookshop made for bookworms. Dark oak shelving, antique lamps, large skylights and galleries running all round combine to transport you to other worlds. The latest novels, histories, biographies and travel guides are arranged by country and invite you to journeys of exploration – at home and comfortably installed on the sofa. There are displays of books which the booksellers recommend.

Der schönste Buchladen der Stadt – wie erfunden für Bücherwürmer. Dunkle Eichenregale, antike Lampen, große Oberlichter und umlaufende Galerien entführen in andere Welten. Die neusten Romane, Geschichtsbücher, Biografien und Reiseführer sind nach Ländern geordnet und laden ein zu Entdeckungsreisen – zu Hause und ganz bequem auf dem Sofa. Displays zeigen die Bücher, welche die Buchhändler empfehlen.

La plus belle librairie de la ville – un endroit privilégié tout trouvé pour les rats de bibliothèque. Des étagères de chêne, des lampes antiques, de lumières d'en haut et des galeries qui longent les murs transportent dans d'autres mondes. Les tout derniers romans, les livres d'histoires, les biographies et les guides de voyage sont classés selon les pays et invitent à des voyages de découverte – chez soi et en jouissant du plus grand confort dans son fauteuil. Des écrans indiquent les livres que les libraires recommandent.

La librería más hermosas de la ciudad, como inventada para ratones de biblioteca. Unas estanterías oscuras de roble, unas lámparas antiguas, unas claraboyas grandes y unas galerías que se extienden alrededor del local transportan a unos mundos distintos. Las novelas más recientes, libros de historia, biografías y guías de turismo se encuentran ordenadas por países e invitan a realizar viajes de descubrimientos desde el propio hogar y cómodamente sentado en el sofá. Unas pantallas colocadas muestran los libros que los propios libreros recomiendan a los clientes.

Fortnum & Mason

181 Piccadilly
London, W1A 1ER
Westminster
Phone: +44 / 20 / 77 34 80 40
www.fortnumandmason.com

Opening hours: Mon–Sat 10 am to 8 pm, Sun noon to 6 pm (with browsing time from 11.30 am to noon)
Products: Food, home, beauty, fashion
Tube: Green Park, Piccadilly
Map: No. 30

Lydia Hearst's Special Tip
The place to go and experience a traditional English tea. This exclusive store is worth a visit.

Tasteful and with historic charm, Fortnum & Mason is much more than a grocery shop. Closely connected with British high society, the enterprise which was established in 1707 by William Fortnum and Hugh Mason supplied even the royal family. Traditional wedding cakes, delicately filled luxury picnic hampers, quality loose teas, Fortnum's Honey – F & M offers shopping with first-class entertainment.

Gediegenheit und historischer Charme – Fortnum & Mason ist viel mehr als ein Lebensmittelgeschäft. Fest verbunden mit der britischen High Society belieferte das 1707 von William Fortnum und Hugh Mason gegründete Unternehmen sogar die königliche Familie. Traditionelle Hochzeitstorten, delikat gefüllte Luxus-Picknickkörbe, exzellente lose Blatttees, Fortnums Honig – F & M bietet Shopping mit Entertainment der Extraklasse.

Une bonne qualité alliée au charme de l'histoire – Fortnum & Mason est bien davantage qu'une épicerie. Fermement associé à la « High Society » britannique, l'entreprise fondée en 1707 par William Fortnum et Hugh Mason fournissait même la famille royale. F & M offre le plaisir des achats combiné à un divertissement de haut niveau qu'il s'agisse de tartes de noces traditionnelles, de paniers de pique-nique luxueux délicieusement remplis, d'excellentes feuilles de thé et de miel Fortnum.

Probidad y atractivo histórico, Fortnum & Mason es mucho más que una simple tienda de comestibles. Estrechamente relacionada con la alta sociedad británica la empresa fundada en 1707 por William Fortnum y Hugh Mason ha suministrado productos incluso a la familia real. Tartas de boda tradicionales, cestas lujosas para meriendas campestres rellenadas con productos delicados, excelentes tés de hoja suelta, miel Fortnum: F & M ofrece Shopping con Entertainment de clase extra.

Harrods

87–135 Bromton Road
London, SW1X 7XL
Knightsbridge
Phone: +44 / 20 / 77 30 12 34
www.harrods.com

Opening hours: Store Mon–Sat 10 am to 8 pm, Sun noon to 6 pm, Food Halls Mon–Sat 9 am
to 9 pm, Sun noon to 6 pm
Products: Anything one requires can be purchased by Harrods on one's behalf
Tube: Knightsbridge
Map: No. 31

Russell James' Special Tip
The world's largest department store sells everything from tea to Burberry bags to crystal dog collars.

This haunt of the rich and beautiful in Knightsbridge is one of the oldest, architecturally most impressive and most luxurious department stores in the world and is a sight in its own right. In 330 departments on seven floors this temple to shopping offers almost anything the heart might desire. Those who are less wealthy come simply to observe or buy a few small items, for instance in the famous deli.

Dieser Treffpunkt der Reichen und Schönen in Knightsbridge ist eines der ältesten, architektonisch beeindruckendsten und luxuriösesten Kaufhäuser der Welt und eine wahre Sehenswürdigkeit. In 330 Abteilungen auf sieben Stockwerken bietet dieser Einkaufstempel fast alles, was das Herz begehrt. Wer weniger reich ist, kommt nur zum Schauen oder kauft ein paar Kleinigkeiten, zum Beispiel in der berühmten Feinkostabteilung.

Ce lieu de rencontre des personnes riches et belles à Knightsbridge fait partie des grands magasins les plus anciens, les plus luxueux et les plus impressionnants sur le plan architectonique dans le monde entier et représente ainsi une véritable curiosité. Dans 330 rayons sur sept étages, ce temple de la consommation offre presque tout ce que l'on peut désirer. Ceux qui sont moins riches se contentent de venir ici rien que pour le plaisir de regarder ou n'achètent de petites choses, par exemple, dans le célèbre rayon d'épicerie fine.

Este punto de reunión de la gente rica y bella en Knightsbridge es uno de los almacenes comerciales más antiguos, más impresionantes arquitectónicamente y más lujosos del mundo, así como un verdadero monumento digno de verse. En 330 departamentos repartidos por siete plantas ofrece este templo de las compras prácticamente todo lo que uno puede desear. El que tiene poco dinero se acerca simplemente para echar un vistazo o para comprar algunas menudencias, por ejemplo en el famoso departamento de comestibles finos.

National Geographic Store

83–97 Regent Street
London, W1B 4E1
Westminster
Phone: +44 / 20 / 70 25 69 60
www.nationalgeographic.com

Opening hours: Mon–Wed+Fri 9 am to 7 pm, Thu+Sat 10 am to 8 pm, Sun noon to 6 pm
Products: Branded clothing, footwear, stationery, maps, travel books, home furnishings and an upmarket travel agent
Tube: Piccadilly Circus, Oxford Circus, Green Park, Leicester Square
Map: No. 32

Inspired by cultures from across the globe, the National Geographic Store brings the whole world together in one extraordinary and versatile place that is much more than a conventional store. It is constantly expanding its range of goods and services, kit the traveller out, and enhance the experience of discovering new worlds.

Angeregt durch die vielfältigen Kulturen der Erde, vereint der National Geographic Store die ganze Welt an einem außergewöhnlichen und vielseitigen Ort, der viel mehr als ein konventioneller Laden ist. Beständig werden die Produktpalette und die angebotenen Features erweitert, Reisende ausgerüstet und die Entdeckung neuer Welten gefördert.

Stimulé par la diversité des cultures dans le monde, le National Geographic Store rassemble le monde entier dans un lieu inhabituel aux multiples facettes qui ne saurait être confondu avec un magasin conventionnel. Les gammes de produits et les services offerts sont constamment étendus : les voyageurs y sont équipés de pied en cap et la découverte de nouveaux mondes est ainsi à l'ordre du jour.

Estimulada por las variadas culturas existentes en la tierra reúne la National Geographic Store la totalidad del mundo en un lugar polifacético y extraordinario, que es algo más que una simple tienda. Constantemente se amplía la gama de productos y los servicios que se ofrecen, se equipa a los viajeros y se promocionan los descubrimientos de nuevos mundos.

Puma Store

51–55 Carnaby Street
London, W1F 9QE
Westminster
Phone: +44 / 20 / 74 39 02 21
www.puma.com

Opening hours: Mon–Sat 10 am to 7 pm
Products: Clothing, footwear, accessories
Tube: Oxford Circus, Piccadilly Circus
Map: No. 33

The first Puma flagship store in Great Britain offers the entire range of clothing, shoes and lifestyle articles by the renowned manufacturer of branded sport and casual fashion. Thanks to collaboration with the Formula 1 Ferrari Team, the avid fan also finds the ultimate Racing Team lifestyle fashion here.

Der erste Puma Flagship-Store in Großbritannien bietet das komplette Sortiment an Bekleidung, Schuhen und Lifestyleartikeln des renommierten Markenherstellers für Sport- und Freizeitmode. Als ein Resultat der Zusammenarbeit mit dem Ferrari-Team der Formel 1 findet der begeisterte Fan hier auch die ultimative Lifestyle-Fashion des Racing Teams.

Le premier magasin phare Puma en Grande-Bretagne offre un assortiment complet de vêtements, de chaussures ainsi que d'articles de Lifestyle de cette marque renommée d'articles réservées aux activités de sport et de loisir. Les fans enthousiasmes de Ferrari trouveront ici le style et la mode de cette écurie de course : c'est le résultat d'une coopération entre Puma et ce constructeur renommé.

La primera tienda de bandera Puma en Gran Bretaña ofrece un surtido completo de ropa, calzado y artículos Lifestyle de este renombrado fabricante de artículos de moda deportivos y de tiempo libre. Como resultado de la colaboración con el equipo Ferrari de fórmula 1 encontrará también aquí el admirador entusiasta las últimas tendencias de la moda del equipo de Racing.

Rococo Chocolates

45 Marylebone High Street
London, W1U 5HG
Marylebone
Phone: +44 / 20 / 79 35 77 80
www.rococochocolates.com

Opening hours: Mon–Sat 10 am to 6.30 pm, Sun 11 am to 4 pm
Products: Chocolate specialities
Tube: Baker Street, Regent's Park
Map: No. 34

Lydia Hearst's Special Tip
Who can resist chocolate? With their decadent, hand-painted and savory treats, Rococo seduces with its passion for chocolate. Their gift hampers are glorious!

This is the most delectable temptation since chocolate was invented: the intoxicating aromas in Chantal Coady's chocolate shop seduce the senses. True to the motto "Good chocolate is like good wine" (healthy in moderation and not to be compared with cheap mass products), in this chocolate Eldorado you find only choice quality made from natural, healthy ingredients.

Dies ist die schönste Versuchung seit es Schokolade gibt: Die berauschenden Aromen in Chantal Coadys Schokoladenladen verführen die Sinne. Getreu dem Motto „Gute Schokolade ist wie guter Wein" – in Maßen gesund und mit billiger Massenware nicht zu vergleichen –, findet man in diesem Schokoladen-Eldorado nur ausgesuchte Qualität aus natürlichen Zutaten und mit gesunden Inhaltsstoffen.

Depuis que le chocolat existe, cet endroit représente la plus belle tentation imaginable : les arômes enivrants dans le magasin de Chantal Coady séduisent les sens. Il reste fidèle à la devise « le chocolat est comme un bon vin ». Il est bon pour la santé lorsqu'il est utilisé de façon mesurée et ne saurait être comparé à une marchandise bon marché. C'est pourquoi on ne trouvera dans cet Eldorado du chocolat que des qualités choisies aux ingrédients naturels et aux additifs sains.

Se trata de la tentación más hermosa desde que existe el chocolate: los embriagadores aromas de la tienda de chocolate de Chantal Coady seducen los sentidos. De acuerdo con el lema de "el chocolate bueno es como el vino bueno" –es sano saludable si se consume de manera comedida y no se puede comparar con los productos baratos que se fabrican al por mayor–, únicamente encontrará en este Eldorado del chocolate calidades seleccionadas fabricadas con ingredientes naturales y saludables.

The Tea House

15 Neal Street
London, WC2H 9PU
Covent Garden
Phone: +44 / 20 / 72 40 75 39
www.covent-garden.co.uk/sites/theteahouse

Opening hours: Mon–Wed 10 am to 7 pm, Thu–Sat 10 am to 8 pm, Sun 11 am to 7 pm
Products: Teas, herbal teas, tea pots
Tube: Covent Garden, Leicester Square, Tottenham Court Road
Map: No. 35

What an aroma! More than 70 types of tea exude tantalising fragrances, from the classic English-blended Earl Grey to the exotic Gunpowder from China. Only best-quality teas are on offer, and the owner's comprehensive knowledge about her great passion, tea, guarantees that the customer will find exactly the right type. Besides teas from all over the world, the tea-lover will also find a wide selection of the necessary accessories.

Dieser Duft! Mehr als 70 Sorten Tee verströmen betörende Wohlgerüche – vom Klassiker English-blended Earl Grey bis zum Exoten Gunpowder aus China. Es sind nur beste Qualitäten im Angebot und die umfassenden Kenntnisse der Inhaberin über ihre große Leidenschaft, den Tee, garantieren, dass der Kunde genau das Passende findet. Neben Tees aus aller Welt findet der Liebhaber hier aber auch das nötige Zubehör in einer vielfältigen Auswahl.

Cet arôme ! Plus de 70 sortes de thés exhalent des senteurs enivrantes – du thé anglais classique English-blended Earl Grey au thé exotique chinois Gunpowder. Seulement les meilleures qualités de thés trouvent place dans cette offre. De plus, les connaissances très étendues ainsi que la passion de la propriétaire garantissent que le client trouvera exactement ce qui lui convient. En plus de thés en provenance du monde entier, l'amateur pourra acheter aussi ce dont il a besoin grâce à une sélection d'accessoires très variée.

¡Qué aroma! Más de 70 clases de té expanden sus agradables olores seductores, desde el clásico English-blended Earl Grey hasta el exótico Gunpowder de China. Solamente se ofrecen los productos de mejor calidad, y los amplios conocimientos de la propietaria sobre algo que constituye su gran pasión, el té, garantizan que el cliente pueda encontrar exactamente lo más adecuado. Junto a tés de todo el mundo podrá encontrar también aquí el aficionado un surtido muy amplio de los accesorios necesarios.

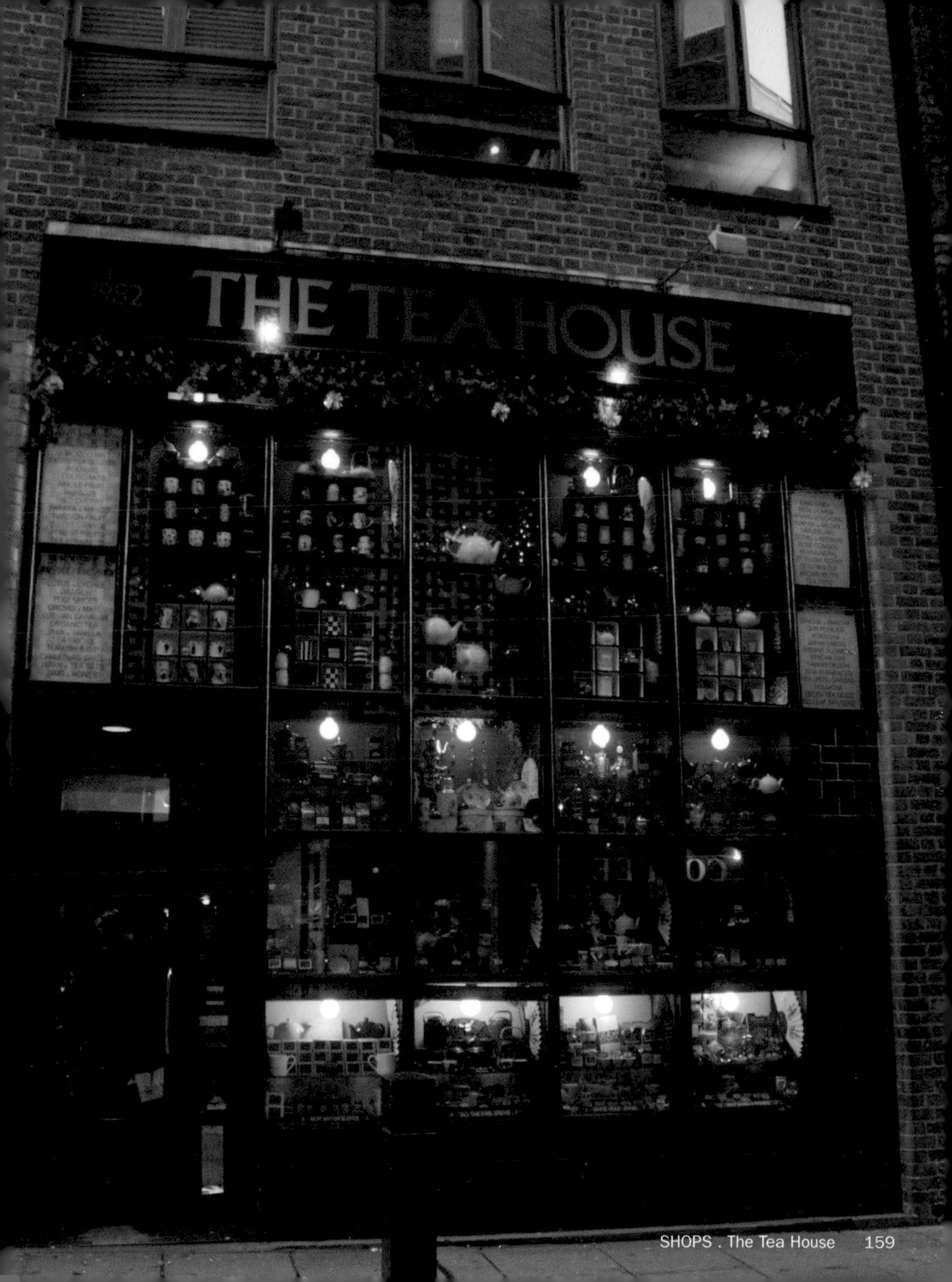
THE TEA HOUSE

HIGHLIGHTS

City Hall

The Queen's Walk
London, SE1 2AA
Bermondsey
Phone: +44 / 20 / 79 83 40 00
www.london.gov.uk

Opening hours: Mon–Fri 8 am to 8 pm and on selected weekends
Tube: London Bridge, Tower Hill
Map: No. 36

An imposing spiral staircase leads into the streamlined glass building designed by star architect Lord Norman Foster. This construction allows scarcely any direct sunlight into the interior, ingenious technology provides air conditioning. Energy needs have been supplied since 2007 by the building's own solar plant. This new landmark has been the official residence of the Mayor of London since 2002.

Eine imposante Wendeltreppe erschließt das Innere des windschnittigen gläsernen Bauwerks von Stararchitekt Lord Norman Foster. Diese Konstruktion lässt kaum direkte Sonnenstrahlung ins Innnere, eine ausgeklügelte Technik sichert die Klimatisierung. Deren Energiebedarf wird seit 2007 aus einer eigenen Solaranlage gespeist. Seit 2002 ist dieses neue Wahrzeichen Amtssitz des Londoner Bürgermeisters.

Un escalier imposant en colimaçon relie les différentes parties à l'intérieur de cette construction aérodynamique en verre conçue par l'architecte en vogue Lord Norman Foster. Cette construction laisse à peine pénétrer les rayons directs du soleil. La climatisation est assurée par une technique sophistiquée. Depuis 2007, les besoins en énergie du bâtiment sont couverts par une installation solaire intégrée. Depuis 2002, ce nouveau symbole de la ville est la résidence officielle du maire de Londres

Una imponente escalera de caracol abre el interior de esta construcción acristalada aerodinámica del famoso arquitecto Lord Norman Foster. Esta construcción apenas permite una irradiación solar directa del interior, encargándose una sofisticada técnica de garantizar la necesaria climatización. Su consumo energético se alimenta desde 2007 de una instalación solar propia. Este nuevo símbolo es, desde 2002, la residencia oficial del alcalde de Londres.

Design Museum

Shad Thames
London, SE1 2YD
Bermondsey
Phone: +44 / 20 / 74 03 69 33
www.designmuseum.org

Opening hours: Daily 10 am to 5.45 pm
Ticket service: www.ticketweb.co.uk
Tube: London Bridge, Tower Hill
Map: No. 37

Russell James' Special Tip
This Thames River institution exhibits the brightest ideas in design, from graphics to furniture to industrial.

Design is at home here. This is made immediately apparent by the building's elegant white facade. The Conran Roche architectural office revitalised a former warehouse as a design temple in 1989. The museum presents temporary exhibitions with a great public appeal that cover all areas of design, from graphic design and architecture to everyday objects and fashion. An absolute must for all design aficionados.

Hier ist Design zu Hause. Das zeigt schon das elegante weiße Äußere des Baus. Das Architekturbüro Conran Roche hauchte 1989 einem ehemaligen Lagerhaus neues Leben als Designtempel ein. Das Museum zeigt publikumswirksame Wechselausstellungen zu Themen aus allen Designbereichen – von Grafikdesign und Architektur über Alltagsgegenstände bis hin zur Mode. Ein unbedingtes Muss für alle Designbegeisterte.

Ici le design se trouve dans l'espace qui lui revient. C'est ce que l'extérieur élégant blanc du bâtiment manifeste d'emblée. En 1989, le bureau d'architecte Conran Roche a insufflé une nouvelle vie à cet ancien entrepôt pour en faire un des temples du design. Le musée montre des expositions temporaires très remarquées sur tous les thèmes de ce domaine : du design graphique et de l'architecture aux objets du quotidien, sans oublier la mode. Une obligation pour tous les passionnés du design.

En este lugar se encuentra el diseño en el entorno adecuado. Esto se aprecia ya contemplando el elegante exterior de la construcción en color blanco. El estudio de arquitectura Conran Roche insufló en 1989 una nueva vida al antiguo almacén convirtiéndolo en el templo del diseño. El museo muestra exposiciones mundiales sobre temas relacionados con todos los aspectos del diseño, desde el diseño gráfico y la arquitectura, pasando por objetos de uso diario, y llegando hasta la moda. Una visita obligada para todos los amantes del diseño.

Hayward Gallery

Southbank Centre
Belvedere Road
London, SE1 8XX
Southwark
Phone: +44 / 20 / 79 21 08 13
www.southbankcentre.co.uk

Opening hours: Daily from 10 am to 6 pm, Tue+Wed to 8 pm, Fri to 9 pm
Admission: Approx. £ 8, price varies depending on the exhibition
Ticket service: +44 / 870 / 1 69 10 00
Tube: Waterloo, Embankment, Charing Cross
Map: No. 38

Anyone who has an interest in contemporary art must visit The Hayward. The concrete block with its crude, cumbersome appearance provides a first-class location for up to four sensational exhibitions a year. The gallery was completed in 1968 as the last building of the Southbank Centre on the war-ravaged South Bank of the Thames. It was named after Sir Isaac Hayward who was a chairman of the London County Council.

Wer sich für zeitgenössische Kunst interessiert, kommt am The Hayward nicht vorbei. Der roh wirkende, sperrige Betonklotz bildet einen erstklassigen Rahmen für bis zu vier aufsehenerregende Ausstellungen im Jahr. Die Galerie wurde 1968 als letztes Gebäude des Southbank Centre am kriegszerstörten südlichen Ufer der Themse vollendet. Ihr Namensgeber, Sir Isaac Hayward, war Vorsitzender des London County Council.

Celui qui s'intéresse à l'art contemporain ne saurait manquer The Hayward. Ce bloc de béton, qui occupe l'espace et impressionne ainsi l'observateur offre un cadre de premier choix à quatre expositions sensationnelles chaque année. La galerie a été achevée en 1968 comme dernier bâtiment de la Southbank Centre sur la rive sud de la Tamise détruite par la guerre. La personne dont elle porte le nom, Sir Isaac Hayward, était le président du London County Council.

Quien esté interesado por el arte contemporáneo no dejará de visitar a The Hayward. El voluminoso bloque de hormigón, de aspecto basto, forma un marco de primera clase para la presentación de hasta cuatro espectaculares exposiciones al año. La Galería se terminó en 1968 como último edificio del Southbank Centre en la ribera sur del Támesis destruida durante la guerra. El nombre se lo debe a Sir Isaac Hayward, un Presidente del London County Council.

London Aquarium

County Hall
Westminster Bridge Road
London, SE1 7PB
Southwark
Phone: +44 / 20 / 89 32 56 55
www.londonaquarium.co.uk

Opening hours: Daily 10 am to 6 pm, July–Sept to 7 pm
Admission: £ 8.25, children 3–14 years £ 6.75, families (2 adults + 2 children) £ 28
Tube: Waterloo, Westminster
Map: No. 39

From the arrow-swift shark to the sideways-scuttling crab – more than 500 species display themselves in over 50 aquariums on three floors. The London Aquarium is one of Europe's largest aquariums. This extensive view of the underwater world is supplemented by varied information about the institute's participation in programmes of active nature conservation and environmental education in British schools and in the media.

Vom pfeilschnellen Hai bis zur seitwärts trippelnden Krabbe – mehr als 500 Arten tummeln sich in über 50 Aquarien auf drei Ebenen. Das London Aquarium ist eines der größten Aquarien Europas. Ergänzt wird dieser ausführliche Blick in die Unterwasserwelt durch vielfältige Informationen zur Beteiligung des Instituts an Programmen des aktiven Naturschutzes und der Umwelterziehung an britischen Schulen und in den Medien.

Du requin rapide comme une flèche au crabe se déplaçant en trottinant sur le côté – plus de 500 espèces différentes s'ébattent dans plus de 50 aquariums sur trois étages. Le London Aquarium est un des plus grands de toute l'Europe. Cette vue détaillée dans le monde sous-marin est complétée par des informations variées concernant la participation de l'institut à divers programmes : qu'il s'agisse de la protection active de l'environnement ou de l'éducation écologique dans les écoles et les médias britanniques.

Desde el rapidísimo tiburón hasta el cangrejo que camina lateralmente a pequeños pasos pueden contemplarse aquí más de 500 especies que se mueven en más de 50 acuarios ubicados en tres niveles. El London Aquarium es uno de los mayores de Europa. Esta contemplación minuciosa del mundo submarino se completa con diversas informaciones sobre la participación del Instituto en programas de protección activa de la naturaleza y de educación sobre el medio ambiente en escuelas británicas y en los medios de comunicación.

Richmond Park

Holly Lodge
London, TW10 5HS
Richmond
Phone: +44 / 20 / 89 48 32 09
www.royalparks.gov.uk

Opening hours: Summer 7 am to sunset, winter 7:30 am to sunset
Tube: Richmond Station
Map: No. 40

No one normally travels to London to observe deer, but some 650 free-roaming animals live in this the largest of London's Royal Parks with an area of 1000 hectares – in the middle of the vibrant metropolis. Wooded hills, ponds, endless paths for cycling and walking, playgrounds and meadows with imposing ancient trees offer opportunities to take a relaxing break from everyday life and to engage in sport and other activities.

Üblicherweise fährt man nicht nach London, um Rehe und Hirsche zu beobachten, aber in dem mit 1000 Hektar größten der königlichen Parks in London leben etwa 650 frei laufende Tiere – inmitten der pulsierenden Metropole. Bewaldete Hügel, Teiche, endlose Rad- und Wanderwege, Spielplätze und Wiesen mit imposanten alten Bäumen bieten Gelegenheit für entspannende Pausen vom Alltag und Möglichkeiten für Sport und andere Aktivitäten.

Normalement, on ne va pas à Londres pour observer des chevreuils et des cerfs. Pourtant, 650 animaux vivent librement – au beau milieu de cette métropole trépidante – dans le plus grand parc de Londres qui ne compte pas moins de 1000 hectares. Des collines boisées, des étangs, des voies cyclables et des sentiers de randonnées interminables, des terrains de jeux, des prés et de vieux arbres imposants offrent la possibilité de se détendre du quotidien et de pratiquer des sports ou de se livrer à d'autres activités.

Generalmente no se desplaza uno hasta Londres para contemplar corzos y ciervos, pero en el parque real de Londres, con una extensión de 1000 hectáreas, viven unos 650 animales en libertad, en el centro de esta palpitante ciudad. Unas colinas cubiertas de bosques, unos interminables senderos y carriles para bicicletas, unas zonas de juegos y praderas con imponentes árboles antiguos permiten disfrutar de relajadas pausas frente al ajetreo diario y ofrecen la posibilidad de practicar deportes y otras actividades.

Royal Opera House

Bow Street
London, WC2E 9DD
Covent Garden
Phone: +44 / 20 / 73 04 40 00
www.roh.org.uk

Opening hours: Mon–Sat 10 am to 3.30 pm plus performance times
Tube: Covent Garden
Map: No. 41

The Royal Opera House is the home of three world class performing companies – The Royal Ballet, The Royal Opera and The Orchestra of the Royal Opera House. It is a focal point for national and internation-al artistic excellence, where the evolving traditions of opera and ballet are taken to the highest levels. From its iconic building, renowned stars and rising talent inspire diverse audiences around the world.

Das Royal Opera House ist die Heimstätte dreier Weltklasseensembles: des Royal Ballet, der Royal Opera und des Orchesters des Royal Opera House. Es bildet einen Kristallisationspunkt nationaler und internationaler künstlerischer Spitzenklasse, der dazu beiträgt, die Traditionen von Oper und Ballett auf höchstem Niveau weiterzuentwickeln. Von dieser ikonenhaften Institution ausgehend, begeistern berühmte Stars und aufstrebende Talente ein vielfältiges Publikum auf der ganzen Welt.

Le Royal Opera House abrite, sous un même toit, trois ensembles de niveau mondial : le Royal Ballet, le Royal Opera et l'orchestre du Royal Opera House. Point de rencontre où se cristallise la fine fleur des artistes nationaux et internationaux, il contribue ainsi à faire évoluer les traditions de l'opéra et du ballet au niveau le plus élevé. De cette institution au caractère « d'icône », des vedettes célèbres et des talents montants enthousiasment les publics les plus différents dans le monde entier.

La Royal Opera House es el hogar de tres conjuntos de renombre mundial: el Royal Ballet, la Royal Opera y la orquesta de la Royal Opera House. Constituye un centro de cristalización de un exponente artístico de primera clase, tanto nacional como internacional, que contribuye a seguir desarrollando las tradiciones de la ópera y el ballet al máximo nivel. Artistas famosos ya consagrados y prometedores talentos, que han salido de esta Institución iconográfica, embelesan a un público muy diverso por todo el mundo.

Shakespeare's Globe Theatre

21 New Globe Walk
London, SE1 9DT
Southwark
Phone: +44 / 20 / 79 02 14 00
www.shakespeares-globe.org

Opening hours: Theatre April–Oct, guided tours all year round
Ticket service: +44 / 20 / 74 01 99 19
Tube: Mansion House, Cannon Street, London Bridge, Southwark, Blackfriars
Map: No. 42

As in Shakespeare's time, theatre performances take place in the open air in the inner courtyard of the timbered building. Outside the performance season from April to October, there is a permanent exhibition and guided tour of the theatre as well as a programme of public events including staged readings, storytelling, lectures and workshops.

So wie einst zu Shakespeares Zeiten finden hier die Theateraufführungen im Innenhof des Holzbaues unter freiem Himmel statt. Außerhalb der Spielzeit von Mai bis Oktober gibt es eine Dauerausstellung und Führungen durch das Theater sowie öffentliche Veranstaltungen wie Bühnenlesungen, Geschichtenerzählungen, Vorträge und Workshops.

Des représentations théâtrales ont lieu dans la cour intérieure et sous le ciel dans l'enceinte de cette construction en bois, tout comme autrefois, à l'époque de Shakespeare. En dehors de la saison, de mai à octobre, une exposition permanente se tient dans le théâtre où sont aussi organisées des visites guidées ainsi que des manifestations publiques telles que des lectures, des conférences et des ateliers.

Del mismo modo que en la época de Shakespeare siguen representándose obras de teatro bajo el cielo en el patio interior de esta construcción de madera. Fuera de la época de representaciones, que se extiende desde mayo hasta octubre, se realizan exposiciones permanentes y visitas guiadas por el teatro, organizándose también actos públicos que consisten en la lectura de obras de teatro, narraciones de cuentos, conferencias y workshops.

Tate Modern

Bankside
London, SE1 9TG
Southwark
Phone: +44 / 20 / 78 87 88 88
www.tate.org.uk

Opening hours: Sun–Thu 10 am to 6 pm, Fri+Sat 10 am to 10 pm
Admission: Free, except special exhibition
Tube: Southwark, Blackfrias
Map: No. 43

Russell James' Special Tip
The onetime power station is a modern-art powerhouse, featuring the best and boldest international artists.

The leading gallery of modern art in Great Britain radiates the brittle charm of an industrial building. In the year 2000 a power station on the South Bank of the Thames, which until 1982 was still generating electricity, became the home of an art collection with international works of the period housing sculptures, paintings, installations from 1900 to the present day. Exhibits by Picasso, Warhol and Dalí are represented here alongside many others.

Die führende Galerie moderner Kunst in Großbritannien versprüht den spröden Charme eines Industriebaus. Aus einem Kraftwerk am Südufer der Themse, das noch bis 1982 Strom erzeugte, wurde im Jahr 2000 die Heimat einer Kunstsammlung mit internationalen Werken aus der Zeit von 1900 bis zur Gegenwart – Skulpturen, Bilder, Installationen. Exponate von Picasso, Warhol und Dalí sind neben vielen anderen hier vertreten.

La galerie leader d'art moderne en Grande-Bretagne a le charme austère d'un bâtiment industriel. Une collection d'art moderne rassemblant des œuvres internationales allant de 1900 jusqu'à l'art contemporain a trouvé place dans cette ancienne centrale électrique située sur la rive sud de la Tamise qui, jusqu'en 1982, produisait encore du courant. Cette collection réunit des sculptures, des tableaux et des installations. On trouvera parmi beaucoup d'autres des œuvres de Picasso, de Warhol et de Dalí.

La Galería de arte moderno más importante de Gran Bretaña imprime su impronta sobre el áspero atractivo de una construcción industrial. A partir de una central eléctrica situada en la margen sur del Támesis, y que seguía produciendo todavía electricidad en 1982, se diseñó en el año 2000 el hogar de una colección de obras de arte que incluye obras desde 1900 hasta la actualidad; en este lugar se pueden contemplar esculturas, cuadros, instalaciones, obras y piezas de Picasso, Warhol y Dalí, junto a muchas otras.

WWW.TATE.ORG.UK

The London Eye

Westminster Bridge Road
London, SE1 7PB
Lambeth
Phone: +44 / 870 / 500 06 00
www.londoneye.com

Opening hours: Oct–May daily 10 am to 8 pm, June–Sept 10 am to 9 pm
Tube: Waterloo, Westminster
Map: No. 44

The world's tallest observation wheel has stood in London since the year 2000. The Millennium Wheel, as it is also known, revolves on the South Bank of the Thames as if it were measuring the minutes of a new era. The glass capsules hover at a height of 135 metres, offering a superb view of London's timeless architecture. Both Londoners and tourists love this central landmark.

Das höchste Aussichts-Riesenrad der Welt steht seit dem Jahr 2000 in London. Das Millennium Wheel – wie es auch genannt wird – dreht sich am südlichen Ufer der Themse, als würde es hier die Minuten eines neuen Zeitalters messen. Die gläsernen Kabinen schweben auf 135 Meter Höhe und bieten einen grandiosen Blick auf Londons zeitlose Architektur. Londoner und Touristen – alle lieben dieses zentrale Wahrzeichen.

La grande roue la plus haute du monde se trouve à Londres depuis l'an 2000. Millenium Wheel – c'est ainsi qu'elle est aussi appelée – tourne sur la rive sud de la Tamise comme si elle mesurait, de là, les minutes d'une nouvelle époque. Les cabines de verre vont jusqu'à 135 mètres de hauteur et découvrent un panorama grandiose sur l'architecture classique de Londres. Les touristes tout aussi bien que les londoniens apprécient ce nouveau symbole de la ville.

La noria panorámica más alta del mundo se halla instalada desde el año 2000 en Londres. La Millennium Wheel –tal y como también se la llama– gira en la margen sur del Támesis como si quisiera medir los minutos de una nueva época. Las cabinas acristaladas flotan a una altura de 135 metros y ofrecen una vista espectacular de la arquitectura intemporal de Londres. Tanto los londinenses como los turistas muestran su afecto por este símbolo central.

The Regent's Park

The Store Yard
Inner Circle
London, NW1 4NR
Westminster
Phone: +44 / 20 / 74 86 79 05
www.royalparks.gov.uk

Opening hours: Daily 5 am to sunset
Tube: Regent's Park, Great Portland Street, Baker Street, St John's Wood, Camden Town
Map: No. 45

Russell James' Special Tip
London's lush, grassy jewel is packed with cricket pitches, rose gardens, winding paths and even a zoo.

The fantastic Rose Garden was laid out as early as 1811 by John Nash; today it is a highlight of the 166-hectare Regent's Park with more than 30,000 rose bushes and 400 varieties. A new feature is the Community Wildlife Garden which was designed, implemented and planted in 2007 with the help of London schoolchildren and volunteers.

Der fantastische Rosengarten wurde bereits 1811 von John Nash angelegt – heute ist er mit mehr als 30.000 Rosensträuchern und 400 Sorten ein Highlight des 166 Hektar großen Regent's Park. Neu ist der Community Wildlife Garden, der 2007 mit Hilfe Londoner Schüler und ehrenamtlicher Helfer entworfen, realisiert und bepflanzt wurde.

Cette roseraie fantastique a été aménagée dès 1811 par John Nash – aujourd'hui elle compte plus de 30.000 plants et de 400 sortes de roses différentes et constitue l'un des centres d'intérêt du Regent's Park dont la surface s'étend sur quelques 166 hectares. Le jardin commun des amis de la nature a été créé récemment : il a été conçu, réalisé et planté en 2007 par des élèves et des étudiants londo-niens ainsi que des bénévoles.

La fantástica rosaleda fue delineada ya en 1811 por John Nash; actualmente constituye un highlight del Regent's Park de 166 hectáreas de extensión con más de 30.000 rosales y 400 especies distintas. Es nuevo el jardín colectivo de amigos de la naturaleza que se diseñó, se materializó y se plantó en 2007 con ayuda de escolares londinenses y ayudantes que intervinieron a título honorífico.

Westminster Cathedral

42 Francis Street
London, SW1P 1QW
Westminster
Phone: +44 / 20 / 77 98 90 55
www.westminstercathedral.org.uk

Opening hours: Daily opens shortly before the first Mass of the day to 7 pm, Sun closes after 7 pm Mass
Tube: Victoria
Map: No. 46

Simply sit still and forget the bustle of the city while contemplating the fascinating colour mosaics. This island of tranquillity is in the heart of the city and is the largest Catholic church in the UK. Many still consider this masterpiece by architect John Francis Bentley, built in early Christian Byzantine style and completed in 1903, to be an insider's tip.

Einfach still sitzen und bei der Betrachtung der faszinierenden farbigen Mosaike den Trubel der Stadt vergessen. Diese Insel der Ruhe befindet sich im Herzen der Stadt und ist die größte katholische Kirche im Vereinigten Königreich. Das 1903 fertiggestellte Meisterwerk im frühchristlich-byzantinischen Stil des Architekten John Francis Bentley ist für viele noch immer ein Geheimtipp.

Oublier l'agitation de la ville en contemplant de fascinantes mosaïques de couleurs. Cette île de paix se trouve au centre de la ville, c'est la plus grande église catholique du Royaume Uni. Ce chef d'œuvre terminé en 1903 dans le style byzantin des débuts du christianisme conçu par l'architecte John Francis Bentley constitue encore une révélation pour beaucoup.

Para quedarse sencillamente sentado y en reposo, olvidando el ajetreo del a ciudad con la contemplación de los fascinantes mosaicos de colores. Esta isla de la tranquilidad se encuentra en el corazón de la ciudad y es la mayor iglesia católica del Reino Unido. Esta obra maestra que fue terminada en 1903 en el estilo bizantino del cristianismo temprano por el arquitecto John Francis Bentley continúa siendo para muchos un verdadero descubrimiento.

DOMINE · JESU · REX · ET · REDEMPTOR
PER · SANGUINEM · TUUM · SALVA · NOS

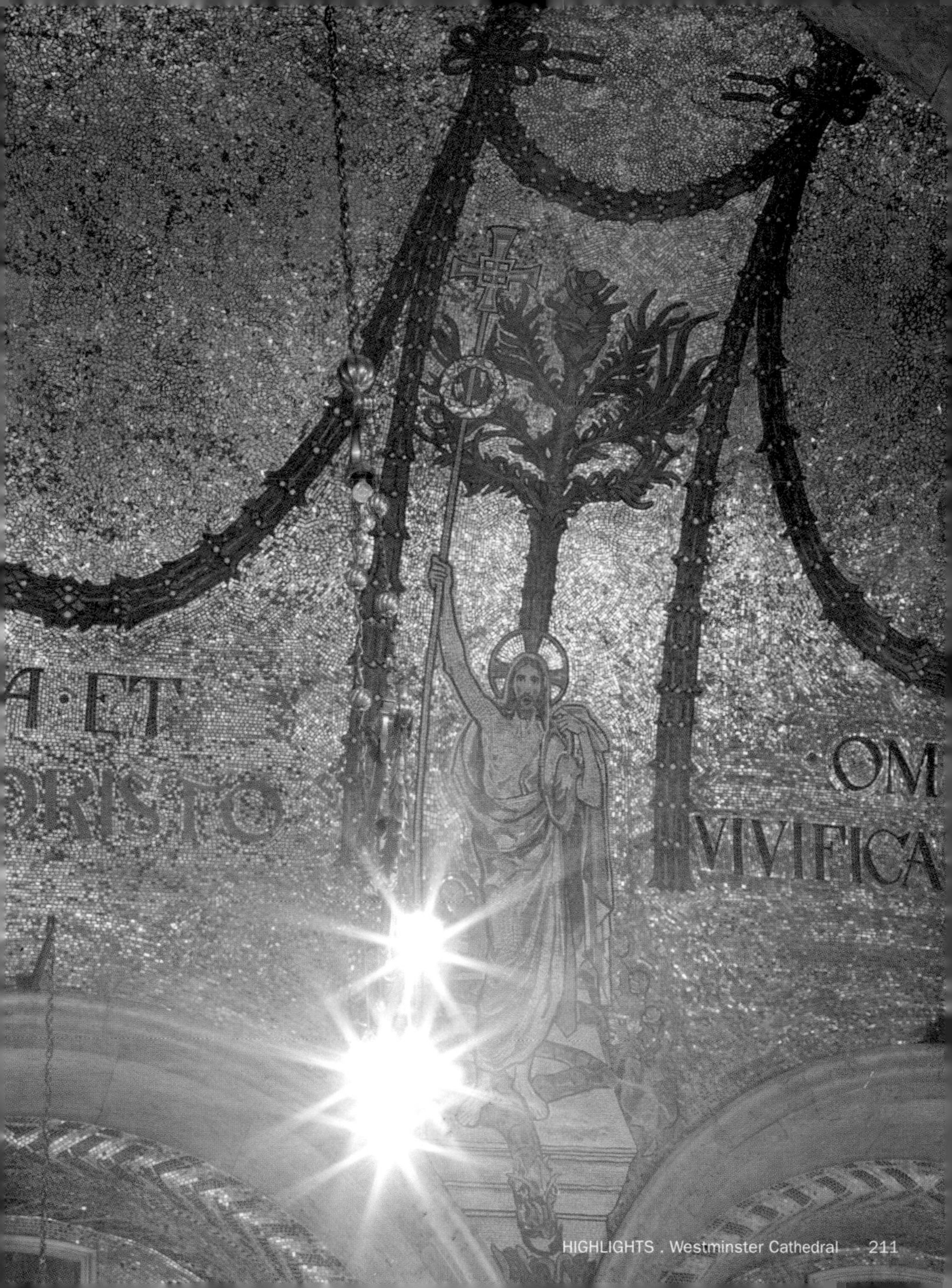
A·ET
CRISTO
·OM
VIVIFICA

ARRIVAL IN LONDON

By Plane
There are five international airports within a radius of 50 km (31 miles) of London.

City Airport (LCY)
Phone: +44 / 20 / 76 46 00 88
www.londoncityairport.com
Situated in the Docklands about 10 km (6 miles) east of the City of London. Served by the Docklands Light Railway (DLR) to and from Bank Underground Station, travelling time 22 mins approx., or 10 mins to and from Canning Town Underground Station, and from there with the Jubilee Line to and from Westminster Underground Station, travelling time 15 mins approx. By the DLR to and from Canary Wharf Underground Station, travelling time 15 mins approx., and from thence by the Jubilee Line to and from Westminster Underground Station, travelling time 15 mins approx. By taxi to and from Central London, travelling time 40 mins approx. at a cost of £ 20 approx.

Gatwick (LGW)
Phone: +44 / 87 00 00 24 68
www.gatwickairport.com
Situated about 42 km (26 miles) south of London. By the Gatwick Express rail link every 15 mins to and from Victoria Terminus Station, travelling time 30–35 mins approx. www.gatwickexpress.com, or by Southeastern Trains, travelling time 35 mins, www.southeasternrailway.co.uk. Also by First Capital Connect every 15 mins to and from London Bridge Station and Kings Cross Terminus Station, travelling time 30–45 mins, www.firstcapitalconnect.co.uk. Cheapest option is by coach with National Express Coaches, departing every 60 mins, travelling time 90 mins, www.nationalexpress.com. By taxi to and from Central London, travelling time 70 mins approx at a cost of £ 80 approx.

Heathrow (LHR)
Phone: +44 / 87 00 00 01 23
www.heathrowairport.com
Heathrow Airport, situated 22 km (14 miles) west of Central London, served by scheduled flights. By the Heathrow Express rail service to Paddington Terminus Station every 15 mins, travelling time 15 mins, www.heathrowexpress.com. Cheaper option is by London Underground, every 5 mins, travelling time 60 mins, www.thetube.com. By taxi to and from Central London, travelling time 60 mins at a cost of £ 40 to 50 approx.

Luton (LTN)
Phone: +44 / 15 82 / 40 51 00
www.london-luton.co.uk
Situated about 53 km northwest of the London Area. From the airport, free shuttle buses to and Luton Airport Parkway Rail Link Station, by services from and to Kings Cross Terminus Station, travelling time 35–50 mins, www.firstcapitalconnect.co.uk. Every 20 mins bus services by from easyBus, GreenLine or National-Express to and from London, travelling time 60–80 mins. By taxi to and from Central London, travelling time 70 mins at a cost of £ 80 approx.

Stansted (STN)
Phone: +44 / 87 00 / 00 03 03
www.stanstedairport.com
Stansted airport, situated about 49 km (30 miles) northwest of London, is mainly frequented by low-budget airlines. Every 15 mins with Stansted Express Rail Link to London Liverpool Street Terminus Station, travelling time 45 mins, www.stanstedexpress.com. Several departures every hour. By bus with National Express Coaches, Terravision Express Shuttle and Terravision Airport Shuttle to London, travelling time from 55 mins. By taxi to and from Central London, travelling time 70 mins approx. at a cost of £ 80 approx.

By Train

A direct rail link service through the Channel Tunnel from Paris Gare du Nord Terminus Station, Brussels Midi or Zuid Stations, or from Lille Europe Station London St. Pancras International.

Phone: +44 / 8705 / 18 61 86, www.eurostar.com or www.raileurope.co.uk. There are eight rail terminus stations in London: Charing Cross, Euston, Kings Cross, Liverpool Street, Paddington, St Pancras, Victoria and Waterloo. All terminal stations have direct access to the London Underground services. Train services are provided by a variety of train operators.

Further Railway Information

National Rail Phone: +44 / 84 57 / 48 49 50 and +44 / 20 / 72 78 52 40 (when calling from continental Europe), www.nationalrail.co.uk

Immigration and Customs Regulations

European Union Citizens require a valid identity card for travel to the UK. For E.U. Citizens there are virtually no custom regulations. All persons of over years of age are allowed tax free for personal consumption: 3,200 cigarettes, 200 cigars, 3 kg of tobacco, 10 litres of spirits, 90 litres of wine and 110 litres of beer.

INFORMATION

Tourist Information

Visit Britain
Thames Tower
Blacks Road
London W6 9EL
Phone: +44 / 20 / 88 46 90 00
www.visitbritain.com

Visit London – Britain & London Visitor Centre (BLVC)

1 Lower Regent Street

Email: blvcenquiry@visitlondon.com
http://eu.visitlondon.com
Mon–Fri: 9 am to 6.30 pm, Sat/Sun: 10 am to 4 pm (Sep to 5 pm) The BLVC is run by the official British Tourism Organization Visit Britain. Free information and advice are available, and also services such as tickets sales, currency exchange and souvenirs. Other Tourist Information Centres (TIC) are located in all airports and at some rail stations, such as:

Waterloo Terminus Station, Arrival Hall daily 8.30 am to 10.30 pm
Liverpool Street Terminus Station, daily 8 am to 6 pm
Heathrow Airport, Terminals 1 to 3, daily 8 am to 6 pm

City Magazines

Published Tuesdays: **Time Out** provides tips on eating out and events for the whole week (available at newsstands). **What's on**, also published on Tuesdays, but less broad. On Thursdays, the **Evening Standard** supplement informs on events. The supplement of the **Guardian** and other national daily newspapers in Saturday editions. **Time Out Eating & Drinking** is useful for choice of restaurants, **Time Out Bars, Pubs and Clubs** informs on the bars scene, **Time Out Shops and Services** gives information on where to shop.

Websites

www.visitlondon.com – Website of London's Tourist Information with events calendar and an online ticket shop
www.london.gov.uk – The London Mayor website and information on London
www.bbc.co.uk/london – News from the BBC
www.londontown.com – Tourist information with several services such as events calendar, hotel bookings

Going out

www.latenightlondon.co.uk – Information on clubs and bars with links
www.squaremeal.co.uk – Restaurant guide
www.thisislondon.co.uk – Leisure Guide of the Evening Standard Daily Newspaper with a large calendar of events
www.timeout.com/london – Restaurants, bars and much more, as well as an extensive cultural programme.

Arts and Culture

www.english-heritage.org.uk – Information on historic buildings, monuments etc., all round Great Britain.
www.officiallondontheatre.co.uk – Events calendar, theatres, tickets
www.royal.gov.uk – Official website of the British Government providing information on Royal Residences and art collections

Sports and Leisure

www.citiskate.com – Every Friday inline skating in Hyde Park
www.ascot.co.uk – Ascot racecourse website

Map

www.london.citysam.de – Interactive London Area map
www.streetmap.co.uk – Address finder with London Area map

Accommodation

www.bhronline.com – Agency for hotel rooms
www.hotels-london.co.uk – London hotels in all price ranges and special offers
www.lhslondon.com – Agency for rooms in guest houses in London

www.londonbb.com – Bed & Breakfast offers in London
www.perfectplaces.co.uk – Apartments, also for long-term tenancies
www.visitlondonoffers.com – Reservation service of the London Tourist Information

RECOMMENDED LITERATURE

Peter Ackroyd
London: The Biography. Ackroyd, one of Britain's most eminent novelists, describes London in his work as a living organism, with its own laws of growth and change.

Monica Ali
Brick Lane. Nazneen, 19 from Bangladesh, is forced into an arranged marriage and finds herself in Brick Lane, the Little India of London's East End. This is a novel about the multicultural life in the East End of London.

Joseph Conrad
The Secret Agent: A Simple Tale. Greenwich and Soho are the principal sets of the criminal case that is set at the turn of the 20th century.

Charles Dickens
Oliver Twist. The classic of world literature describes the story of the orphan Oliver Twist and points out the appalling state of social affairs in Victorian London.

Samuel Pepys
The Diaries of Samuel Pepys. The collection provides a definitive eyewitness account on the years between 1660–1669. It offers detailed insight in intrigues and scandals as well as historical descriptions of the coronation of Charles II, the Plague and the Great Fire of London in 1666.

CITY TOURS

Sightseeing Tours

By Bus and Underground

Central London and a several boroughs of the London Area can be visited at a modest price by public transport, i.e. by the **bus line Riverside 1**, on the south side of the Thames departing from Catherine Street, Aldwych via County Hall and Tate Modern Gallery towards Tower Bridge and Tower Hill. Architecture and design fans can head for the tube stations designed by top architects by the **Jubilee Line**. **Sightseeing Double-Decker Bus** – double-decker bus services with an open upper deck circulate every 10 to 30 mins through Central London, hop on/off is possible at all bus stops. Daily 8.30 am to 6 pm, 24 hour season ticket, £ 18 approx.

Big Bus Company

Phone: +44 / 20 / 72 33 95 33
www.bigbus.co.uk

Original London Sightseeing Tour

Phone: +44 / 20 / 88 77 17 22
www.theoriginaltour.com

Black Taxi Tours

Phone: +44 / 20 / 79 35 93 63 or
+44 / 7956 / 38 41 24, www.blacktaxitours.co.uk
Black taxi tours address individual demands. Max. 5 passengers, for 2 hours. £ 100

Pedicabs

Bicycle taxis seating from 2–3 passengers, with cab stands at various sites, provide rides through central London.

Boat Tours

Sightseeing

Goods views of riverside Central London are obtained from the Thames. Cruises depart all year round from Westminster Pier downstream towards Greenwich and the Thames Flood Barrier, and during the summer season upstream via Kew and Richmond towards Hampton Court. Additional special cruises. Tickets from £ 10.00 approx., and discounts with valid Travel Cards.

Bateaux London Phone: +44 / 20 / 76 95 18 00
www.catamarancruisers.co.uk
City Cruises Phone: +44 / 20 / 77 40 04 00
www.citycruises.com
Thames River Boats Phone: +44 / 20 / 79 30 20 62
www.wpsa.co.uk
London Duck Tours Phone: +44 / 20 / 79 28 31 42
www.londonducktours.co.uk
Yellow amphibious vehicles offer combined sightseeing, by road and on the River Thames, daily departure at the London Eye, duration 75 mins approx., from £ 19.

Canal tours

Barge trips along the Regents Canal from 'Little Venice', London Zoo and Camden Lock.
London Waterbus Company Phone: +44 / 20 / 74 82 26 60, www.londonwaterbus.com
Jason's Trip Phone: +44 / 20 / 72 86 34 28
www.jasons.co.uk

Guided City Tours

Private City Guides
Blue Badge Guides
Phone: +44 / 20 / 74 95 55 04
www.tourguides.co.uk
Tailor-made tours and visits.

Theme tours

2-hour walking tours as an introduction to the Roman history of London, through those parts of London immortalised by Shakespeare, Sherlock Holmes, or Jack the Ripper or during evening pub crawls.

Original London Walks

Phone: +44 / 20 / 76 24 39 78, www.walks.com

Architectural Guided Tours

Architectural Dialogue

Phone: +44 / 20 / 73 80 04 12
www.architecturaldialogue.co.uk
Every Sat 10 am approx. 3-hour tour.

Silver Jubilee Walkway

www.jubileewalkway.com
On the occasion of Queen Elizabeth II Coronation Jubilee, a long walk of 23 km (14 miles) on both sides of the River Thames between Tower Bridge and Lambeth Bridge was developed. From the starting point in Leicester Square, the crown signs showing the direction of the route is to be followed. A map is available at museums and tourist information centres.

Outlook Points

British Airways London Eye

www.ba-londoneye.com
A gradual 30 minute flight in the high-tech glass cabins of the world's tallest observation wheel (135 m/ 440 ft) Sept daily 10 am to 9 pm, Oct–May to 8 pm, Fare: £ 15.50.

Ex-Natwest-Tower/Tower 42

25 Old Broad Street
www.tower42.com
Wonderful views can be enjoyed by guests in the ex-

clusive 'Vertigo 42' Champagne Bar on the top floor. Mon–Fri noon to 3 pm, 5 pm to 10 pm.

Tower Bridge

www.towerbridge.org.uk
Breathtaking views from the Walkways over the River Thames and the riverbank through special viewing windows. April–Sept daily 10 am to 6.30 pm, Oct–March daily 9.30 am to 6 pm, £ 6

St Paul's Cathedral

www.stpauls.co.uk
The dome galleries offer fascinating views of London. Mon–Sat 8.30 am to 4 pm, £ 10

TICKETS & DISCOUNTS

Ticket Offices

Ticketmasters

Phone: +44 / 870 / 534 44 44
Phone: +44 / 161 / 385 32 11 (when calling from outside the UK), www.ticketmaster.co.uk
Ticket Centre: Greenwich Tourist Information, 2 Cutty Sark Gardens, Greenwich, Mon–Sat 10 am to 4.30 pm

Stargreen

20/21 A Argyll Street
London W1F 7TT
Phone: +44 / 20 / 77 34 89 32
www.stargreen.co.uk
Mon–Fri 10.15 am to 7 pm, Sat. 10.15 am to 6 pm

tkts – Half Price Ticket Booth

Leicester Square, Mon–Sat 10 am to 7 pm, Sun noon to 3 pm. Canary Wharf, DLR station, Mon–Sat 10 am to 3.30 pm. Last minute sales, discount theatre tickets for same-day performances – most tickets are disposed of at half price. www.officiallondontheatre.co.uk/tkts

Discounts

London Pass

Free admission without waiting time to more than 50 Sites, as well as discounts on city tours and events, in restaurants and recreational facilities etc. Can be combined with a Travel Card for free bus and train journeys. The pass can be purchased online at www. londonpass.com or at the Britain and London Visitor Centre. One day: £ 39 and/or £ 46 incl. Travel Card, two days: £ 52 and/or £ 66, three days: £ 63 and/or £ 83, six days: £ 87 and/or £ 129

Travel Card

Travel Cards are valid for travel on all public transportation. They are available for one, three or seven days. Peak fares are valid all day, Off Peak fares Mon–Fri from 9.30 am and all day on Sat/Sun and public holidays. The Visitor Travel Card is valid for the internal Zones 1+2 within which most sites are located. Travel Cards can be purchased in advance at a travel agency or online at Visit Britain, www.visitbritain.com, basic price: £ 7

Oyster Card

The new Oyster Card comes with a rechargeable chip. The fares for trains and buses is paid electronically. All tickets are half price. The card can be purchased in advance online at Visit Britain, basic price: £ 14.50

GETTING AROUND IN LONDON

Local Public Transport

Transport for London

Phone: +44 / 20 / 72 22 12 34 (24 hour service)
www.tfl.gov.uk

Information concerning the London Underground, Docklands Light Railway, buses and Thames ferries. Information concerning the Line Network can be downloaded from the TfL website. Travel Information Centres are at located at Heathrow Airport, at London Underground stations, such as at Victoria, Liverpool Street and Piccadilly Circus. The **London Underground** is the fastest and most comfortable means of transport in London, and also connects to Greater London. The core of the Network is the 'yellow' Circle Line, which connects the main train stations. In recent years, the Network has been extended by the Jubilee Line and the Docklands Light Railway. Trains operate Mon–Sat 5.30 am to 12.30 am, Sun 7.30 am to 11.30 pm. Tickets are available from ticket offices or from ticket machines. Tickets are retained until the end of the journey to pass through the ticket barriers. The London Underground Network has six Zones for fare charging purposes. Single tickets for Zone 1 cost £ 4. The London Underground Network is complemented by a dense **Bus Network**. Night buses are marked with a blue "N" in front of the line number. There are two different types of bus stop: one is a white sign on a red circle where buses always halt and the others are request bus stops with a red sign on a white circle where buses will only halt on request by hand signal. Tickets are available from ticket machines at the bus stops. Single fare: £ 1.60. Cheaper travel is possible with Travel Cards or Oyster Cards (see above). These are valid for one day and more.

Taxis

Phone: +44 / 871 / 871 87 10 and
+44 / 20 / 72 72 02 72,
Phone: +44 / 87 / 00 70 07 00 (only available from mobile phones)

FESTIVALS & EVENTS

Chinese New Year
End Jan/beginning Feb, parades, dragon dances, fireworks in China Town.

Oxford and Cambridge Boat Race
Beginning of April, rowing regatta of the two universities between Putney and Chiswick Bridge (www.theboatrace.org)

Easter Sunday Parade
Mar/April, fair and parade at Battersea Park.

London Marathon
Mid/end April, from Greenwich to St James's Park (www.london-marathon.co.uk).

Summer Exhibition
At the beginning of June–mid Aug, exhibition of contemporary British artists at the Royal Academy (www.royalacademy.org.uk).

Trooping the Colour
The second Sat in June usually is the official birthday of the monarch with a tattoo parade.

Wimbledon Lawn Tennis Championships
End June/beginning July, on a couple of weeks, international tennis championships (www.wimbledon.org).

City of London Festival
End June–mid July, during several weeks, city festival with music, dance and theatre performances (www.colf.org).

Pride Parade
At the beginning of July, gay and lesbian parade from Hyde Park towards Victoria Embankment (www.pridelondon.org).

Greenwich & Docklands International Festival
Every weekend in July, open-air dance, theatre and music performances along the River Thames (www.festival.org).

BBC Henry Wood Promenade Concerts ("The Proms") Mid July–mid Sept, series of concerts in the Royal Albert Hall that rounds off with the patriotic Last Night of the Proms Concert (tickets should be booked in advance, www.bbc.co.uk/proms).

Notting Hill Carnival
Last weekend in Aug, Afro-Caribbean festival, Sun 'Children's Day Parade', Mon 'Main Parade' (www.nottinghillcarnival.org.uk).

Mayors Thames Festival
Over one weekend each year in Sept, an amusement park and street theatre is held along the River Thames; together with many highly decorated boats (www.thamesfestival.org).

London Open House Weekend
Third weekend in Sept, free access to old and new buildings normally closed to the public (www.londonopenhouse.org).

Great River Race
Beginning of Sept, boats race, with Dragon and Viking boats, from Ham House towards Isle of Dogs, with entertainment (www.greatriverrace.co.uk).

Trafalgar Day Parade
Sun before and/or after 2nd Oct, commemorating and in honour of the naval hero Admiral Horatio Nelson held at Trafalgar Square with a parade of the Royal Navy on Horse Guards Parade. Guy Fawkes Day 5th Nov, in commemoration of the foiled gunpowder to blown up King James I and his Parliament in 1605, accompanied by firework displays and bonfires in a many parks around the London Area with a real festive atmosphere (www.bonefire.org).

USEFUL NOTES

Electricity
Voltage 240 Volt. British electrical outlet sockets take three poles plugs. Adapters required for typical Europe dual pin plugs.

Money

National currency: the British Pound Sterling
1 British Pound (£) = 100 Pence (p)
Exchange rate (as off spring 2009):
£ 1.00 = EUR 1.10 approx.
EUR 1.00 = £ 0.90 approx.
Euros and Dollars can be changed in banks and bureaux de change offices, whereby bureaux de change offices generally have a more disadvantageous exchange rate. When Euros are accepted, change will be given in £. **Bank and credit cards:** Maestro cards or credit cards can be used to draw cash at cash machines (ATMs). Most restaurants and shops accept credit cards.

Emergency

Emergency Hotline: Phone: 999 (police, fire, ambulance and fire brigade)

Opening Hours

Banks: Mon–Fri 9.30 am to 3.30 pm, in shopping malls opening hours to 5.30 pm as well as Sat 9.30 am to 1.30 pm. Bureaux de change offices are open daily. **Shops:** Mon–Sat 9 am/10 am to 6 pm/7 pm, Thu to 8 pm. Major supermarkets are open to 10 pm, some are open 24 hours daily. Several shops and stores open on Sundays: noon to 6 pm. **Museums:** 10 am to 5/6 pm, closing day varies. **Restaurants:** Lunch approx. noon to 2 pm, dinner approx. 7 pm to 10 pm. **Pubs:** from the end of 2006, there is no legal closing time; pubs can open 24/7. **Costs & Money** London is really expensive. Accommodation rates for a double room inclusive breakfast, start at £ 65 for B&B and a budget hotel. Online bookings are in general much cheaper. An entrance to an exclusive bar or café starts at about £ 12, in restaurants at least £ 20; takeaways are a cheaper alternative.

Smoking

Smoking is prohibited in enclosed public places, pubs, bars and restaurants.

When to go

The climate is mild and unsettled. Winters are generally snow-free, with predominantly crisp winds and wet and cold weather conditions.

Telephone

STD Area Code within the U.K. and London: 020
Calls from abroad: +44 + required STD Area Code without zero
Calling from London: country code + area code without zero, + required telephone number
Operator Service National: dial 100, international: dial 155
Directory Enquiries: Phone: 11 85 00
The 8-digit local numbers for Central London require the prefix '7', and in Greater London, the prefix '8'. In cases of failed connections, use the operator. Most of the old red telephone boxes are out of use. The new, mostly glass telephone booths function with coins, phone cards or credit cards; phone cards are available from newsstands.

Tipping

A 10–15 % tipping surcharge is normal in restaurants if service charge is not included. In pubs you pay at the bar; tipping is unusual. Tipping is expected from taxi drivers, tourist guides, hairdressers and hotel staff.

Time

Great Britain has Greenwich Mean Time (GMT) which is an hour behind Continental Europe. Summer time (+ one hour between March and October), corresponding with the Continent.

No.	Location	Page
1	Boxwood Café	16
2	Canteen Spitalfields	20
3	Cocoon Restaurant	24
4	Fifteen	28
5	Hakkasan	32
6	Le Pain Quotidien	36
7	Moro	40
8	Nicole's	44
9	Nobu Berkeley ST	48
10	Sake No Hana	52
11	Salt Yard	56
12	St Alban	60
13	The Zetter Restaurant	64
14	Tom's Delicatessen	68
15	Wahaca	72
16	1707 Wine Bar	78
17	Adventure Bar & Lounge	82
18	Artesian Bar	86
19	Buddha Bar	90
20	Ghost Inc	94
21	Mamounia Lounge	98
22	The Loft	102
23	Westbourne House	106
24	Bamford & Sons	112
25	Borough Market	116
26	Camden Market	120
27	Coco de Mer	122
28	Covent Garden	126
29	Daunt Books	132
30	Fortnum & Mason	136
31	Harrods	140
32	National Geographic Store	146
33	Puma Store	150
34	Rococo Chocolates	154
35	The Tea House	158
36	City Hall	164
37	Design Museum	168
38	Hayward Gallery	172
39	London Aquarium	176
40	Richmond Park	180
41	Royal Opera House	184
42	Shakespeare's Globe Theatre	188
43	Tate Modern	192
44	The London Eye	198
45	The Regent's Park	202
46	Westminster Cathedral	208

teNeues' new Cool Guide series

ISBN 978-3-8327-9293-0

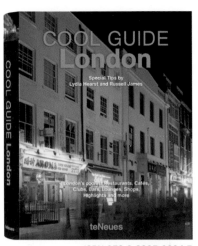

ISBN 978-3-8327-9294-7

ISBN 978-3-8327-9295-4

ISBN 978-3-8327-9296-1

Size: **15 x 19 cm**, 6 x 7 ½ in., 224 pp., **Flexicover**, c. 250 color photographs,
Text: English / German / French / Spanish
www.teneues.com

Other titles by teNeues

ISBN 978-3-8327-9235-0

Size: **25.6 x 32.6 cm**, 10 x 12⅞ in., 396 pp., **Hardcover with jacket**, c. 650 color photographs,
Text: English / German / French / Spanish / Italian
www.teneues.com

Other titles by teNeues

ISBN 978-3-8327-9309-8

ISBN 978-3-8327-9274-9

ISBN 978-3-8327-9237-4

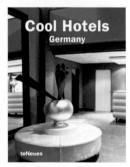

ISBN 978-3-8327-9247-3

ISBN 978-3-8327-9234-3

ISBN 978-3-8327-9308-1

ISBN 978-3-8327-9243-5

ISBN 978-3-8327-9230-5

ISBN 978-3-8327-9248-0

Size: **15 x 19 cm**, 6 x 7 ½ in., 224 pp., **Flexicover**, c. 200 color photographs,
Text: English / German / French / Spanish / Italian
www.teneues.com